365 Self-Care Activities for Women

Your Daily Guide to Well-being

By Sandy R. Ross

Publisher: Book & Bat Publishing

PO Box 820, Indooroopilly, Qld 4068, Australia

Email: info@bookandbat.com

Every effort has been made to ensure the accuracy of the information contained in this book. However, the publisher assumes no responsibility for errors or omissions, or for damages that may result from the use of the information contained herein.

ISBN: 978-1-7636378-1-8

First Edition: August 2024

Printed by Amazon KDP

Legal Notice

Disclaimer Notice

TABLE OF CONTENTS

FROM THE AUTHOR

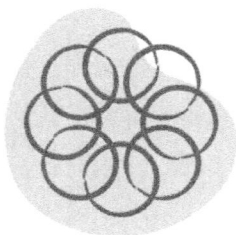

Hello, I'm Sandy Ross, and I'm thrilled to welcome you to 365 Self-Care Activities for Women. This book is close to my heart because it's born from both my personal experiences as a busy woman, and the insights I've gained through my work as a counselor.

Every day, I meet women who are juggling multiple roles—being good humans, mothers, partners, workers, caretakers—and I often hear how hard it is for them to find time for themselves. This book is for you. It's filled with quick, easy activities that fit into your busy life and help you feel better, one day at a time. I believe in the power of taking small steps each day to improve our health and happiness.

Self-care wasn't a huge part of life in my family of origin, and it wasn't until later in life that I started to recognize how important it is for women to put their own needs on the top of their very long to-do lists. I hope these activities become a cherished part of your day and bring you as much joy and peace as they've brought to me.

Warmly,

Sandy Ross

INTRODUCTION

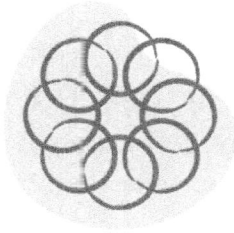

What comes to mind when you think of "self-care"?

Do you picture luxurious spa days, exotic vacations, or extravagant shopping sprees?

Perhaps you think self-care is a privilege reserved for those with plenty of money. Or you may think self-care is good for other people who can afford the time.

Picture this: it's Monday morning. You've just managed to get out of bed, barely sipped your coffee, and the day's demands are already piling up. Your phone is buzzing with emails, your to-do list is growing, your family needs your attention, the dog needs to be walked, and you're wondering if you remembered to pay the utility bills.

On top of that, there's a huge staff meeting you're worried about and that laundry mountain isn't going to fold itself.

As you rush around, you remember you need to schedule a dentist appointment, pick up groceries, and somehow squeeze in a workout. Meanwhile, your friends are texting about the weekend plans.

By the time you finally get to work you're exhausted. And the day has just begun.

In the middle of this, finding even a moment for yourself seems impossible.

But it's the reality for many women. With so many demands on your time and energy, self-care can easily feel like another demand. You know you have to take care of yourself or you will not be able to care for anyone else.

But it can seem like an elusive luxury, something that other people have time for, but you do not. Yet self-care is about more than just surviving the daily grind; it's about thriving and living a fulfilling life.

You Deserve It

We often see self-care in advertisements aimed at women, usually as a way to sell products we don't necessarily need. The "you deserve it" message is often tied to a designer bag, expensive skincare or a pricey household item. It's no wonder many people equate self-care with overspending.

But real self-care is both far easier and more important than we might think. It goes beyond the superficial and taps into our essential needs.

This book can help you reframe what self-care truly means for you as a woman and a person deserving of care, even outside of your roles in other people's lives.

So What Is Self-care?

Self-care is recognizing your needs and making them a priority in your life. This may come easier for some women than others. Research has shown that many women feel obligated to put the needs of children, spouses, parents, friends, and even pets ahead of their own. For them, the concept of self-care can seem foreign or even selfish.

But self-care is not selfish. Self-care is about ensuring your health and happiness so you have the energy and time for the people you love.

You've probably heard the common saying to 'put your oxygen mask on first before helping others.' It borrows from the standard pre-flight announcements; the instruction that if there is a change in cabin pressure, you need to put your mask on first so you can breathe. It's the only way you can help anyone else.

This is true for self-care, too, except you don't have to keep going until your body screams at you to stop before you can begin caring for yourself.

People often say it's good when they have a reason to slow down as it makes them focus on their priorities. It might be due to something like a breakup or illness. It gave them a 'legitimate' reason to slow down, rearrange their priorities, and allocate time and energy to care for themselves. This can happen, and it does, but it need not be your story.

Yes, self-care may be difficult at first. It may be hard because you don't have models in your family structures or work settings of people caring for themselves. Getting examples and then finding support to reinforce those thoughts and behaviors may be challenging. It may take conversations with your spouse and kids about why some things must change, and with your boss about a flexible work schedule. It takes effort at first. But before that, it takes believing that you are worth it. And you are.

That's what this book can show you. It will define self-care, help you set self-care goals, create a self-care toolkit, and then provide you with 365 self-care activities that you can make part of your self-care routine. These self-care activities are designed specifically for busy women like you. Whether you're in your mid-20s navigating the early stages of your career or in your late 50s juggling work and family responsibilities, this book is here to help you prioritize yourself without feeling overwhelmed.

In these pages, you'll discover a treasure trove of self-care practices that can be seamlessly integrated into your daily routine. Some are small, fast, and simple. Some will take more time. Adapt them to your lifestyle, schedule, and unique needs. From physical exercises and emotional well-being practices to tips for social connection and financial stability, you'll find a comprehensive approach to nurturing every aspect of your life.

Each small step you take toward self-care will lead to significant improvements in your overall well-being because self-care is not about perfection, but progress. Even the smallest activity, like taking a moment to breathe deeply or savoring a cup of tea, can make a big difference.

It's a continuous journey, not a one-time achievement. As your life evolves, you'll discover more about yourself—your limits, preferences, and passions—and you will need to adapt your self-care routine. This is why there are no prescriptions here; there are just descriptions and suggestions to make your life easier at every stage.

The activities can fit seamlessly into modern lives, and if this book achieves that for you, it has done its job.

How to Use This Book

This book contains 365 self-care activities across the following realms of self-care:

- Self-care for your body
- Self-care for your mind
- Self-care for your feelings
- Self-care for your soul
- Self-care in your relationships
- Self-care at work
- Self-care with money
- Self-care in your environment

It aims to help you achieve a balanced lifestyle, improved health in all aspects of life, deeper personal connections, enriched mental engagement, and a nurturing personal environment that promotes overall well-being.

It is divided into two parts: the first part is an introduction to self-care and the second is the activities. You'll also find useful references and resources to make it easier to integrate the different activities.

Choosing Activities

The activities in each realm are arranged from the one that takes the least time to do, to the longest. Skim the pages so you know what's possible, then choose a realm to start— whichever one you prefer. For example, if you feel you need to take different care of your body, pick an activity in that section and do it. You can do one each day or combine a few activities to suit your time and head space. And you can move between realms – no need to work all the way through one realm before moving on to the next.

5

Feel free to experiment with different activities until you find the ones that suit your schedule best and leave you feeling cared for. One activity will be suitable for one week but impossible the next because of changes in your schedule. That's perfectly all right. Adjust and move forward. The goal is to take some time for yourself consistently, even if that time varies from day to day.

Some activities take longer and need more resources than others; pick what fits your time and resources. Self-care should not stress you more because you stretched your time or resources.

This book is not intended as a substitute for professional help, but as a guide; think of it as a friend holding your hand. If you find yourself struggling with significant physical or mental health issues, seek support from a mental health or physical health professional. Self-care activities can complement professional treatment but are not a replacement for it.

Start With Just One Thing and Go From There

When you begin practicing self-care, you'll notice positive changes in your life. You'll be more present in all your relationships. You'll reconnect with what makes you unique, feel more energetic, and experience less anxiety and depression.

Try it. Pick an activity and do it. You don't have to read anything else in this book to get started, or wait for a crisis to remind you to care for yourself. Make self-care a daily habit. Breathe in the oxygen every day.

PART I
ALL ABOUT SELF-CARE

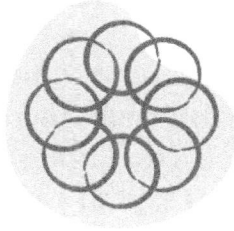

There are a lot of misconceptions about what self-care actually is.

It seems as though people swing between overindulging and not practicing self-care at all.

This first section introduces the perspective that self-care is a mindset, a decision, a lifelong habit.

You will learn what it is, how it came about, how to set sustainable self-care goals and how to track them.

CHAPTER 1
WHAT IS SELF-CARE?

Self-care has become a buzzword in our daily conversations in recent years. According to Google, there were nearly 10 million 'self-care' and related searches in 2022 alone. Research by Worldmetrics expects that by 2025, the self-care market will reach $16.8 billion, up from $13.2 billion in 2017.

This chapter discusses the history of self-care to help you understand how we got here. Then, it defines it and explores its transformative power across eight crucial realms of life. You will understand self-care as a vital component of your well-being, something you do every day, and not just a luxury. And you will see how timeless practices like Kaizen and modern science converge to support your well-being.

A Brief History of Self-Care

The historical path that has shaped our current perception of self-care might reshape your understanding of the term today. A brief look through the #selfcare hashtag on Instagram or TikTok will show you images ranging from sugar scrubs and manicures to inspirational quote cards and breathtaking mountain-top views. These representations owe to how much self-care has evolved to become such a broad term.

The concept of self-care traces is rooted in medical ethics and patient-centered care in the 1950s. It was a response to the increasing recognition that patients needed to take an active role in their own health and well-being. It was a departure from traditional paternalistic medical practices, where doctors made decisions on behalf of patients without much input from the patients.

At first, self-care was started in mental hospitals to promote patients' physical, mental, and emotional health. Institutionalized patients often lack a sense of control over their daily lives. They were encouraged to do simple things like regular exercise, eat well, and do their own personal grooming. These practices were seen as both therapeutic and as ways to restore a sense of autonomy and self-worth to patients.

Self-care as Social Justice

During the civil rights movement in the 1960s and 70s, the concept of self-care gained importance. Marginalized communities, especially African Americans, fought for civil rights and fair access to healthcare.

The Black Panther Party, known for its bold activism, adopted self-care as a vital part of its community efforts. They viewed it as a way to empower themselves and combat systemic racism and inequality. Their healthcare initiatives promoted free services that met both immediate and preventative health needs. They emphasized holistic health practices specifically designed for the needs of underserved communities.

This period marked a significant shift where self-care intertwined with social justice and community empowerment.

As we entered the 1980s, activists like Audre Lorde expanded the conversation on self-care to include intersectional perspectives, particularly highlighting the health challenges faced by Black LGBTQ communities. Lorde famously said, "caring for myself is not self-indulgence, it is self-preservation, and that is an act of political warfare."

The turn of the 21st century brought renewed attention to self-care in response to significant national and global events. The trauma of the 9/11 terrorist attacks led to heightened awareness of mental health and trauma recovery, with self-care practices being integrated into therapeutic approaches for survivors.

This period also coincided with economic recessions that highlighted the importance of personal resilience in dealing with financial instability and uncertainty.

By the 2010s, self-care had transitioned from a niche concept to a mainstream idea. The term "self-care" began appearing more often in popular media and social conversations, thanks to the growing awareness of mental health issues and the focus on the importance of holistic well-being.

The changing political landscape and the COVID-19 pandemic further amplified discussions around self-care, as people looked for strategies to cope with new political and social challenges.

Today, self-care has evolved beyond its activist origins to include digital communities, wellness influencers, and many products and services marketed toward promoting well-being. Social media has made it possible for people to share self-care routines and experiences and created a global conversation about the importance of prioritizing emotional, mental, and physical health.

What about the history of self-care was new to you? Reflect on it. Which parts were the most significant to you?

What Exactly is Self-Care?

We've already discussed that self-care is a vital component of your well-being, and something you do every day. To understand it more deeply, we can take a step back and consider what a human being needs to thrive.

Abraham Maslow proposed a theory of human motivation and needs as a hierarchy. It's a pyramid, with basic needs such as food, water, and shelter as the base. These must be met before progressing to higher-level needs, moving up the pyramid to mental and physical health, relationships, and personal growth. He suggested that the ability to thrive and reach our full potential depends on building a strong base.

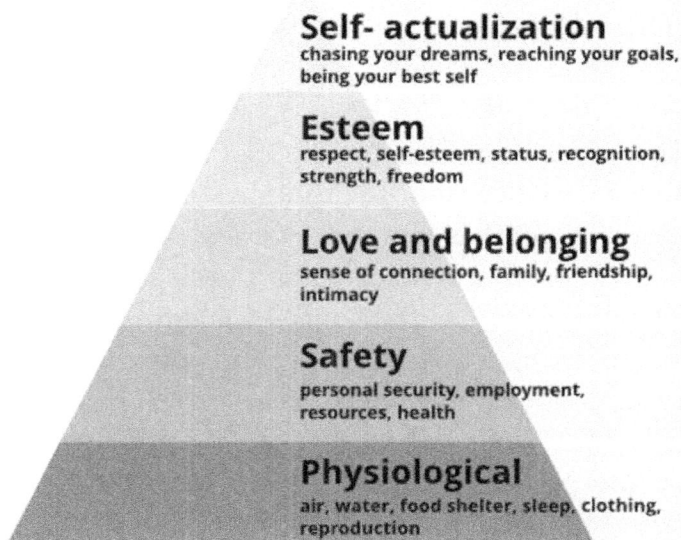

Self- actualization
chasing your dreams, reaching your goals, being your best self

Esteem
respect, self-esteem, status, recognition, strength, freedom

Love and belonging
sense of connection, family, friendship, intimacy

Safety
personal security, employment, resources, health

Physiological
air, water, food shelter, sleep, clothing, reproduction

As he refined his theory, Maslow explained that people prioritize different needs based on their circumstances and personal experiences. For example, some might focus more on feeling respected or achieving goals, while others might prioritize friendships or their creative interests.

When your needs are met you can function well and live a fulfilling life. When they are not met, it can lead to stress, anxiety, and difficulty in managing daily life. For example, if emotional needs like love and belonging are unfulfilled, it can lead to feelings of loneliness or depression.

Self-care is about finding what your needs are and meeting them. When you think of it this way, you can begin to let go of the myth that self-care is selfish. Rather, it is a foundational part of life: when we take care of ourselves, we're better equipped to take care of others and fulfill our responsibilities.

Realms of Self-Care

You can care for yourself across different aspects of life, introduced below. The next part of this book covers each aspect in more detail through activities.

Self-Care For Your Body

Physical activities such as exercise and adequate sleep have been extensively studied for their impact on health and well-being. Research published in the *American Journal of Lifestyle Medicine* found that regular physical activity is associated with many health benefits, including reduced risk of chronic diseases, improved mood, and enhanced quality of life. Self-care for your body includes activities that keep your body operating at optimal levels, such as caring for your skin and your inner health.

Self-Care For Your Mind

A study in the *Journal of Applied Psychology* found that mindfulness practices, for example, reduce stress and enhance focus, contributing to better overall mental health. Activities that stimulate your mind, such as learning new skills or

12

practicing mindfulness, have been shown to improve cognitive function and emotional resilience.

Self-Care For Your Feelings

This is about recognizing and managing your emotions, expressing feelings constructively, and seeking support when you need it. Studies highlight the importance of emotional intelligence in personal relationships and overall life satisfaction. The *Journal of Personality and Social Psychology* suggests that positive social relationships are associated with better mental health outcomes, including reduced stress and increased life satisfaction.

Self-Care For Your Soul

Spiritual fulfillment and meaning, such as meditation, prayer, spending time in nature, or engaging in religious practices are some of the many ways to care for your soul, or your spiritual needs. They promote psychological well-being by fostering a sense of meaning and connection. Research from the *American Psychologist* shows that spirituality can enhance resilience and contribute to mental health.

Self-Care In Your Relationships

Nurturing healthy relationships and maintaining social connections are essential for emotional support and overall happiness. Relationships in this book means all your social relationships, not only with an intimate partner or children. A study in *Health Psychology* notes, "strong social ties are associated with lower levels of depression and anxiety, as well as increased longevity."

Self-Care At Work

Self-care at work is about working without overextending yourself. This can be incredibly hard to do when you're at the foundational levels of Maslow's hierarchy: keeping you and yours fed and sheltered. But, work-life balance and stress management at work contribute to your overall well-being. Research in the *Journal of Occupational Health Psychology* indicates that effective stress management techniques reduce burnout and improve job performance. Being a human is about more than producing for a job.

Self-Care With Money

Making sound financial decisions and managing your money the best way you can helps to reduce financial stress and improve mental health. According to one study in *Psychology & Marketing*, financial well-being is associated with greater life satisfaction and lower levels of psychological distress. Self-care with money involves planning your spending and saving, learning more about money, and making the best financial decisions you can.

Self-Care In Your Space

Our surroundings affect our well-being. Self-care in your space is about creating the most supportive physical environment you can, like keeping your personal areas organized and minimizing clutter, which enhance your mood and productivity. It's so important to your well-being that research (published in *Frontiers in Psychology*) has found that a positive physical environment promotes well-being and reduces stress levels.

Progress Over Perfection: The 1% Rule

By now you might be accepting that self-care is a practice that evolves over time; it is not something you do once and then dispense with. Like any practice, it is also about making progress and not about perfection. In fact, there is no such thing as perfection when it comes to self-care.

You may have heard of the saying 'Rome wasn't built in a day.' This may be ancient wisdom, but it still holds true. It is the basis for a simple but powerful concept called the 1% improvement rule. It states that making small and consistent improvements of 1% every day, can lead to significant growth in your life. In the same way, self-care is about making one small change today.

It may be tempting to make giant changes in a day and go at your self-care goals with your full focus. You might book a visit to a spa, resolve to read a book a week, meditate for an hour a day around your new yoga class. You rearrange your first week to accommodate it but by day 2 find that you have less time today, and on day 3 decide you'll do more tomorrow. Then it's next week and life has overtaken your best intentions. You resolve to try again later.

If you resemble that story, the 1% improvement rule might be the sustainable way forward. By focusing on small steps instead of looking for the perfect routine, you can enjoy the impact of great self-care practices for all your life.

The 1% improvement rule finds its roots in Kaizen, a Japanese approach that emphasizes small consistent continuous improvements as the key to long-term success. Similar to how savings grow exponentially over years through compound interest, consistent, modest improvements in your personal growth create significant progress and transformation.

Examples of the 1% improvement rule can be seen in many areas. Athletes, for example, refine their skills little by little, which leads to better performance overall. Artists improve their craft through small, regular adjustments. In self-care, spending a few minutes each day to care for yourself can make feel you more grounded and improve your overall well-being.

The rule offers many advantages over trying to make big changes all at once. Making small improvements is easier and less overwhelming than trying to completely change your life overnight. It helps you avoid feeling stressed or giving up on your goals. In the next chapter, you will learn how to set achievable self-care goals and how to track your progress.

For now, what new thing have you learned about self-care? Do you resolve to make at least one small change a day?

CHAPTER 2
SELF-CARE GOALS

Self-care goals help you live with intention. As the famous saying goes, if we don't know where we are going, we'll never get there. Self-care goals honor our minds, bodies, and spirits and help us to show ourselves the kind of love we need. They keep us growing in life.

Self-care goals are like personal reminders of how much you value yourself. They're an important first step to infusing a sense of satisfaction into life. How you see, hear, and respect yourself dictates everything else that you do in life. Setting and following through with your self-care goals teaches you how to find balance, and using SMART goals helps you achieve them.

Your happiness and health will never depend on another person, but the way you take care of yourself. Self-care goals bring you back to yourself. They force you to ask:

- Am I being consistent with my needs?
- Am I putting my well-being and health first and foremost?
- Am I giving myself what I need to feel most aligned with my best self?

This chapter will help you define your personal self-care goals to create a focused and intentional plan for nurturing your well-being. It will teach you how to set realistic, achievable objectives that align with your values and lifestyle and empower you to stay committed, and track your progress effectively.

Setting SMART Goals

SMART is an acronym for:

Specific (significant, simple, and sensible)

Measurable (motivating and meaningful)

Achievable (attainable)

Relevant (realistic, reasonable, resource and results-based)

Time-bound (limited by time, timely and time-sensitive)

The thing with goals is that if they are not focused and well-defined, you can spend your life running up and down the field, getting tired and never scoring. They remind you of what is lacking in the moment. This is why they need to be focused. Focus makes goals positive tools.

If you have ever felt like you were working hard but not making progress, it could be that your goals were a little too general. Or, if you ever struggled to see how you fulfill your ambitions, probably your goals needed refining. Many people spend their lives moving between activities or rushing around trying to get things done while accomplishing very little. Setting SMART goals helps you clarify your ideas, keep your efforts focused, use your resources and time productively and increase the chances of achieving the things you want out of life.

The criteria are commonly attributed to Peter Drucker's Management by Objectives concept. It was first used by George T. Doran and later by Professor Robert S. Rubin in an article for The Society for Industrial and Organizational Psychology. Other people have written about and expanded the criteria, but here is the basis for setting SMART goals:

Specific

Your goal needs to be clear and specific otherwise your efforts will be unfocused. When making your goal specific, try to answer the five 'W' questions:

- What do I want to do?
- Why does it matter?
- Who is involved?
- Where do I do it?
- What resources do I need?

Look at the general goal 'I want to be physically fit'. As a SMART goal, to make it specific, you might ask yourself:

- What do I want to do to become fit?
- Why does it matter?
- What aspect of physical fitness do I want to focus on?

The goal would become something like, 'I will run on the treadmill, to increase my endurance.'

Measurable

You need to be able to measure your goals so that you can stay motivated and track your progress. Tracking your progress keeps you focused, helps you meet your deadline and allows you to feel the excitement of getting closer to fulfilling your goal. To make a goal measurable, ask yourself questions like:

- How many?
- How much?
- How will I know when it is done?

For our example about becoming physically fit, you would ask yourself

- How much running do I have to do to build my endurance?
- How will I know when I have gotten there?

Then the goal would become, 'I will run for 15 minutes, three times a week, on the treadmill to increase my endurance.' The goal is now measurable because it specifies the duration of the activity and the frequency. You can track progress by recording the distances you cover over time.

Achievable

A goal needs to be measurable and specific, and also realistic. It should stretch your abilities but should still be possible for you to achieve. One way to make a goal achievable is to look at previously overlooked resources or opportunities that can bring you closer to your goal. To make your goal achievable, ask yourself:

- How can I meet this goal?
- What constraints do I have to overcome?

Back to our example of physical fitness, to make it achievable, you may ask:

- Is running for 15 minutes three times a week practical for me?
- Now that I want to do it on a treadmill, do I have the resources to get a treadmill or a gym membership?

Let's say the answer is no. Then the goal would become, 'I will run for 15 minutes, three times a week, to increase my endurance.'

Tip: Here, be careful not to set goals that someone else has power over. For example, 'get the kids to give me 20 minutes of quiet time in the evening' may not be achievable because it depends on other people. 'Create some quiet time alone in the evening,' completely relies on you, because you can opt to change your environment, for example, to make it possible.

Relevant

This step has to do with connecting your goal to yourself. You want the goal to matter to you and to align with your overall life goals.

Yes, we all need help and support to achieve our goals, but it's important that we maintain control over them. Make sure that even though your self-care goals help others, you are still responsible for achieving them.

To check for relevance, ask yourself the following questions. You want your answer to be yes for all of them.

- Does this goal seem worthwhile?
- Is the timing right?
- Am I the person to be going after this goal?
- Does it match my other needs?
- Does it apply in my current environment?

To make our example relevant, you may ask yourself:

- Is it the right time to be trying to be physically fit?
- Does it seem like a worthwhile goal?

If you choose running for your fitness activity, then 'I will run 15 minutes a day, three times a week, to increase endurance' would be relevant.

Tip: if you have a health condition or a disability, running might not be the best choice. A better physical goal may be some type of swimming or hydrotherapy. Choose activities that work for your unique circumstances.

Time-bound

Every goal needs to have a due date. When you have a deadline, you can focus your efforts appropriately and have something to work toward. The SMART goal criteria help you make sure that daily tasks do not take priority over your longer-term goals. A goal that's time-bound will answer the following questions:

- When?
- What can I do three months or six months from now?
- What can I do in six weeks?
- What can I do today?

Applying these questions to our goal, it may become, 'I will run 15 minutes a day, three times a week, beginning today to increase endurance. I will do this for three months.'

That way, the goal has a schedule and a timeline for achieving milestones and maintaining consistency in habit formation.

SMART Goals Keep You Objective

They provide motivation and help keep your self-care goals in perspective. When you know where your goal line is, you will work to meet it. It will force you out of your comfort zone and keep you going when you are tempted to fall out of habit, which is the topic for the next chapter. For now, what two self-care goals have you been able to identify? Can you make them SMART?

What Self-Care Goals Do I Set?

The most vital self-care goals are often the most obvious. For instance, our baseline is to ensure we all get enough water and sleep, so that other self-care activities are actually effective. But, we also all need to meet our emotional needs.

When setting goals for your self-care, connect with the things you really want out of life. There are so many possibilities available to us, all claiming to have a say in how we do life. It is easy to get distracted by them and imagine you want what others have.

Remember, the essence of self-care is that you meet your needs which are as unique as you are. A good place to start is to ask yourself what fulfills you. Think about the thoughts, words and actions that make you feel most alive. Look at different aspects of life including your work, mental health and personal goals.

Some examples of self-care goals include:

- Take a 10-minute walk outside each day
- Increase my water intake by drinking 8-10 glasses of water each day
- Limit social media use to 30 minutes per day

- Schedule regular check-ins with friends and family
- Avoid overspending and prioritize needs over wants
- Set boundaries with others to protect my energy and time

Tracking Your Self-Care Goals

Tracking your self-care goals keeps you accountable. It allows you to monitor your progress and adjust your approach as needed. If you have successfully made your goal SMART, you already have an idea of how tracking would look.

Identify your metrics

Decide the specific behaviors that you want to track. For our getting fit example, you may want to tick the weeks you actually run for three days.

Metrics for different self-care goals include things like exercise routines, meditation sessions, time spent on an activity, and so forth.

Your metrics can also be outcome-based, tracking things like increased energy, better mood, and reduced stress levels. It will vary based on the self-care goal.

Choose your methods for tracking

You can track your metrics through weekly or daily journals. You can also use apps and technology that are designed for habit formation and goal tracking, you simply log your activities and monitor your progress. Visit www.SandyRossAuthor.com/resources for suggestions.

Be sure to use calendars and planners to schedule and prioritize your self-care activities.

Set the frequency of tracking

Decide how often you want to monitor your progress. For some self-care goals, daily tracking may be suitable, while weekly tracking may work better for others. Use the appropriate frequency.

Make measurable milestones

Using the 1% improvement rule, after doing small activities for a while, you should see results. For example, running 15 minutes a day will improve your endurance which should be noticeable within the first month.

You can set a milestone after the first month, to help you gauge where you are and see if to keep the activity or adjust it a bit. After each milestone, adjust according to need.

Monitor and reflect

Based on your set frequency and milestones, review your tracking data and see how you are doing toward your goals. Reflect on what is working and what needs changing. Factor in your changing circumstances and revise your goals as needed, especially where you constantly fall short of your targets.

Always celebrate your achievements along the way, no matter how small they are. It will help reinforce positive habits.

Example of Goal Tracking

Goal

Improve the quality of your sleep – aim for 7-8 hours of quality sleep per night with consistent bedtime routines.

Tracking Method

Keep a sleep journal to record the time you go to bed, wake up, hours slept and the factors affecting sleep.

Frequency

Track nightly and at the end of each week to identify trends and patterns in sleep quality.

Adjustments

If after two months there is no improvement in sleep quality, adjust bedtime routines and/or seek professional advice.

The biggest benefit of tracking self-care goals is that it will help make it a habit. The goal is to make self-care a routine that supports your overall well-being. You'll see more of this in the next chapter.

For now, pause and reflect; how can you make self-care goals that align with every aspect of your life? How will you track them?

CHAPTER 3

SELF-CARE ROUTINE

Self-care means listening to your body and soul, taking some time to check in and intentionally challenging your belief systems and behaviors when things feel out of alignment.

Anyone who has tried to adopt self-care, especially for the first time in their lives, will tell you that it can be challenging especially when there is a lot going on in the world that you cannot control. This chapter will help you know how to do it. It will provide you with practical strategies to seamlessly integrate self-care into your existing schedule, no matter how busy you are. You'll learn to make self-care a non-negotiable part of your day—a habit for life.

What is a Habit?

By definition, a habit is a routine or behavior that you repeat regularly and often happens unconsciously. Brushing your teeth in the morning is a habit. Fixing a cup of coffee is a habit. A lot of times, you do these things on autopilot because you have repeated them so often that they have become ingrained.

Your life today is basically the sum of your habits. Whether you're fit or out of shape, happy or unhappy, successful or not—it all boils down to what you do repeatedly. What you spend time thinking about and doing every day shapes who you are, what you believe, and how others see you.

The goal here is to make self-care into a habit. That way, self-care will become a natural and normal part of your life. To do this, you have to understand how habits are formed so that you can use that in your favor.

The Habit Loop

Building a habit can be broken down into four simple steps: cue, craving, response, and reward – often called the habit loop. Your brain follows these steps in the same sequence each time.

Cue

The cue is what triggers your brain to start a behavior. It's a signal that predicts a reward. Research shows that back in the day, our ancestors looked out for cues like where to find food, water, or a mate. Today, we're more attuned to cues that predict things like money, fame, love, or personal satisfaction—stuff that indirectly helps us survive and thrive.

Your brain is always scanning your surroundings for hints of where a reward might be. Because the cue is the first sign that a reward is close, it naturally leads to a craving.

Craving

Cravings are the second step in the habit loop. They drive every habit. Without some level of motivation or desire—without wanting to change—there's no reason to act. Generally, we crave the feelings habits give us. You're not motivated by brushing your teeth; you want the feeling of a clean mouth. You don't just turn on the TV; you are craving entertainment. Every craving is about wanting to change how you feel inside.

Of course, cravings vary from person to person. In theory, anything could trigger a craving, but people are motivated by different cues. For a gambler, the sound of slot machines can spark a powerful urge to play. For someone else, those same sounds might just be background noise. Cues don't mean much until they provoke a craving. What turns a cue into a craving depends on your thoughts, feelings, and emotions when you notice it.

Response

This third step is the actual habit you perform—it could be a thought or an action. It is the actual brushing of teeth or eating chocolate or watching TV. Whether you act depends on how motivated you are and how much effort you have to make.

If an action requires more effort than you're willing to give, you won't do it. If you are unable to perform the action, you won't do it.

A habit can only happen if you're capable of doing it. If you dream of dunking a basketball but can't jump high enough, well, you're out of luck.

Reward

After you respond, you get a reward. After you brush your teeth, you get the feeling of a clean mouth. Rewards are what every habit is aiming for.

To break the whole process down: the cue is about noticing that reward. The craving is about wanting that reward. And then, the response is about actually getting that reward.

As a general rule, we chase rewards because they either:

- Make us feel good or
- Teach us something.

Rewards satisfy your craving. Food and water give you the energy to keep going. Getting a promotion means more money and respect. Getting fit improves your health and maybe your love life. But the best thing about rewards is that they satisfy that craving—whether it's for food, status, or approval. They give you a moment of happiness and relief.

Secondly, rewards teach us what's worth doing again. Your brain is always on the lookout for rewards. As you go about your day, your senses are checking out which actions make you happy and which ones don't. Feeling good or disappointed helps your brain decide what's useful and what's not. Rewards close the loop and finish off the habit cycle.

If any part of this cycle is weak, the habit won't stick. Take away the cue, and the habit never starts. Lower the craving, and you won't feel motivated to act. Make the task too hard, and you won't do it. And if the reward doesn't hit the spot, you won't want to do it again. Without the first three steps, a behavior doesn't even happen. And without all four, it sure won't stick. It's this feedback loop that allows you to create automatic habits.

Bear in mind that these four steps happen fast. You have to be mindful to notice a cue before it triggers the craving, for example.

We can split the four steps into two phases: the problem and the solution phase. The problem phase includes the cue and craving. It is when you notice that you need to change something. The solution phase includes the response and the reward. It's when you act to make the change you want to happen.

All behavior is driven by the need to solve a problem. Sometimes, the problem is that you see something good that you want. Other times the problem is that you have a pain you need to relieve. Either way, the habit helps you solve the problems you face.

Here are two examples of the habit loop at work:

Example 1

Cue – Your phone buzzes.

Craving – You want to see who is texting and what it is about.

Response – You pick up your phone and read the text.

Reward – You feel good to have read the text.

As you repeat this process, grabbing the phone gets associated with your phone buzzing.

Example 2

Cue – You wake up.

Craving – You want to feel alert.

Response – You fix a cup of coffee.

Reward – You satisfy your craving to feel awake.

Over time, drinking coffee becomes associated with waking up.

This loop is endless. It is always running and active during every waking moment. The brain is always scanning the environment, predicting what will happen next, experimenting with different responses and adapting. One run round the loop happens in a split second. We use it repeatedly without even realizing.

How to Create New Habits

We can use the habit loop as a framework for forming good habits and getting rid of bad ones. James Clear, the author of *Atomic Habits*, created laws for behavior change based on these four steps. Each law is like a lever that influences how you behave. When the lever is positioned right, you create good habits effortlessly. When it's wrongly placed, it's impossible to create a good habit. These are the four laws:

- Cue – make it obvious
- Craving – make it attractive
- Response – make it easy
- Reward – make it satisfying

You can also invert the laws to break a bad habit.

- Cue – make it difficult to see
- Craving – make it unattractive
- Response – make it difficult
- Reward – make it unsatisfying

Fitting Self-Care into Your Existing Schedule

Every time you want to add a self-care activity to your schedule, (or change any behavior for that matter) ask yourself how you can make it obvious, attractive, easy, and satisfying. Remember, every goal is doomed to fail if it goes against your nature.

The self-care activities in this book are easy to implement. Choose the ones that are attractive, obvious, and satisfying to you and your job will be halfway done. Remember to keep repeating the action. It is repetition that solidifies behaviors into habits. That said, use the following tips to fit self-care into your schedule:

- Prioritize it – Your day may have a lot of to-dos, but self-care needs to be a priority. Treat it as non-negotiable.
- Begin small – Start with small- and manageable-time chunks for self-care. 5-15 minutes a day is a great place to start if you are completely new to self-care.
- Schedule your activities – Treat self-care like an appointment. If you need to, calendar it and set reminders.
- Stay flexible – Adapt your self-care activities when necessary. Don't be too hard on yourself if you miss a day or two.
- Repeat it – You need consistency to make self-care a sustainable habit. You can try performing your activities at the same time every day or week to make it a habit.

Remember to combine it with your daily activities and keep it simple. You don't always have to do elaborate and time-consuming activities when you are short on time. As long as the activity leaves your tank fuller, you have won the day.

In the next chapter, we'll help you prepare a self-care toolkit to make it that much easier, but at the moment, reflect on this: *how can I make a self-care routine that fits my schedule based on the principles of habit formation?*

Chapter 4
Your Self-Care Toolkit

A self-care toolkit is a personalized collection of items and resources that help you feel better when you're feeling distressed or upset. It is filled with things that comfort you when you need it and help you meet your own needs. It's a sort of go-to place for when you need to practice self-care. It's the place you can go without always having to first find the items you need to help you feel better, because it is pre-stocked. This chapter will help you by providing the essential tools and resources for self-care. You will find a self-care starter pack to tweak and make self-care a part of your life.

Why You Need a Self-Care Toolkit

A self-care toolkit makes it easier for you to look after yourself and feel better when you are having a rough time. Rather than scrambling to find ways to boost your mood or deal with stress, the toolkit already has what you need. It helps you when life gets overwhelming and you need a relaxing activity. It makes it easier to take a break from all your daily pressures when things start piling up.

A self-care toolkit is a reminder to prioritize self-care. It can help to bring your attention to what really matters in your life. Besides, building it can be a fun way to get creative and know yourself. You get to pick out different items, make them look and feel cool and relax while at it.

You need a curated list of practical and tangible items to make your self-care routine even better. They will make it easier to incorporate self-care into your daily life.

Self-Care Starter Pack

Everyone's self-care toolkit looks different because we all have different needs and choose different activities. This starter pack list is meant to be a place for you to springboard from. Adjust it to make it your own. Remember to build your toolkit as you try out different self-care activities and to change it as you grow and change. Note that you don't have to spend a fortune on self-care. Most of the things you need in this starter pack or the activities provided later in the book are things that are affordable and readily available.

- Aromatherapy - Essential oils, scented candles, bath salts or bath bombs.
- Skincare - A gentle cleanser, moisturizer, and sunscreen.
- Body care - A loofah, body wash, and lotion.
- Interactive items - Journals, coloring books, or puzzles.
- Books - A book or e-book on a topic you enjoy, mindfulness, or a favorite hobby.
- Tea or herbal infusions - A selection of calming teas or herbal infusions.
- Stuffed animals or comfort objects - A soft toy or comfort objects like pillows and blankets.
- Yoga or exercise equipment - A yoga mat, resistance bands, or a fitness tracker.
- Meditation, tracking, and journaling apps – apps like Headspace or Calm that you can use for guided meditation sessions. You can also keep your journals

online using journaling apps that also help you track your progress.

- Pampering extras – Nail polish or gel, nourishing snacks.

Handling Feelings of Guilt

Many women feel guilty for taking time for themselves, especially if their movement through life so far has been to prioritize everyone else. You're reading this book because you know you need to take time for yourself anyway. These tips can help you recognize and manage any guilty feelings.

Shift your perspective

Remind yourself that self-care is not a luxury. It is you recharging your batteries so that you can care for others. Your phone needs to charge to work, and you need to relax and feel good.

Set boundaries

Sometimes, the feelings of guilt may be intensified by the demands of your loved ones on your time. Let them know that you are having your me-time. It may be difficult for them to grapple with the idea at first. If you persist, you will set an example for them that it's okay to prioritize their well-being too.

Reflect on the benefits of self-care

Notice how you feel after self-care—more focused, happier, and relaxed. Let those be what you dwell on when you are tempted to wallow in guilt. Treat yourself like you would a friend. If your friend needed a break, you would encourage them, right? Give yourself the same encouragement and understanding.

PART II:

SELF-CARE ACTIVITIES

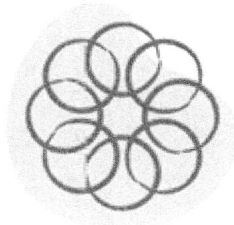

The activities range from simple actions that you can do in an instant, to things you need to do throughout the day. They're affordable, easy to implement, vary in time requirements, and can be scheduled into your busy life.

Some will seem simple or quite obvious: they are. They're probably things you already know you should do, and are often the first things we forget to do. So, see them as reminders of what you don't make time to do.

Not every activity will fit your exact circumstances every day, so adapt them as you need to. For example, you might not have a bath, or prefer to not soak in a tub. You could adapt an activity like this to 'have a long warm or cool shower'.

There's no right or wrong way to 'do' self-care – unless you don't do it at all.

The 1% Rule In Action

Unmet needs or everyday niggles grow when you ignore them, like weeds. But pay attention to the flower bed, notice the weeds poking their heads through the soil, and they pull out easily. If you keep pulling out the weeds, the flowers thrive.

Self-care activities are the same. Small actions taken regularly are a way to make sure you keep your life balanced. And the more you do them, the more the results compound as your habits change to ones that are more nurturing of yourself.

Approach each activity with an open mind, watch how much power they have to transform your life.

CHAPTER 5

SELF-CARE FOR YOUR BODY

Taking care of your body improves your overall quality of life. If you nurture it, you boost your physical health, enhance your energy and vitality. Whichever activities you pick, begin by setting the intention to care for yourself.

You can use an affirmation such as the following to help you:

- My presence is important and valid in this world.
- My body is a precious gift, deserving of care and respect. It is worthy of love in all its forms.
- I am deeply thankful for the incredible things my body enables me to experience and accomplish every day.
- Thank you, my body, for your strength and resilience today.
- I nurture my body with love and respect, and in return, it provides me with the strength and vitality to thrive.

The Activities

1.   Put on a robe

Why: Putting on a cozy robe is a simple act of self-care that instantly wraps you in comfort and warmth. It's like giving yourself a hug and creating a relaxing atmosphere around you.

Time: Less than 5 minutes.

Tools: Comfortable robe.

How: Slip into your favorite robe after a shower, before bed, or whenever you want to unwind. Feel the soft fabric against your skin and embrace the feeling of relaxation it brings.

Did putting on a robe help you feel more relaxed and comfortable? Was it a comforting and nurturing gesture toward yourself?

2.   Drink an extra glass of water

Why: Staying hydrated is essential for overall health and well-being. Research has shown that 70% of the population is mildly dehydrated and unaware of it. Drinking an extra glass of water can boost your energy and support your body's functions.

Time: Less than 5 minutes.

Tools: Drinking water.

How: Keep a water bottle handy throughout the day and aim to drink an additional glass of water beyond your usual intake. Take small sips and hydrate your body to feel refreshed.

Did drinking an extra glass of water make you feel more hydrated and energized? How do you think it will benefit your overall health?

3.   Get dressed in some comfy clean clothes

Why: Getting dressed in comfy, clean clothes is a way to refresh and renew your energy. It sets the tone for a productive day or a relaxing evening ahead.

Time: Less than 5 minutes.

Tools: Comfy clothes.

How: Choose clothes that are soft and comfortable, such as loungewear or your favorite casual outfit. Change into these clothes after a long day or whenever you need a mental reset.

Did changing into comfy clothes improve your mood and mindset? Was it a positive start or end to your day?

4.   Give yourself a scalp massage

Why: Giving yourself a scalp massage is a simple way to enhance your shampoo routine or just to relax your mind. It stimulates blood flow to your scalp, promoting hair growth and reducing stress levels.

Time: Less than 5 minutes.

Tools: Fingertips or handheld scalp massager.

How: Use your fingertips to gently massage your scalp in circular motions. Start from the front of your hairline and work your way toward the back of your head. Continue massaging for about 60 seconds to reap the benefits.

Did the scalp massage help you feel more relaxed or rejuvenated?

5.   Moisturize your body with your favorite lotion

Why: Moisturizing your body is a nourishing self-care ritual that hydrates your skin and leaves it feeling silky smooth. Choose a lotion that is rich in antioxidants and nourishing oils.

Time: Less than 5 minutes.

Tools: Your favorite lotion.

How: After showering or bathing, apply lotion all over your body, focusing on dry areas like elbows and knees. Gently massage into your skin until fully absorbed. Enjoy the aroma and the immediate softness it provides.

Did moisturizing leave your skin feeling moisturized and healthy? Was it a soothing and pleasant experience?

6.   Do a 5-minute meditation

Why: Meditation can reduce stress and enhance focus. It promotes a sense of calm and well-being.

Time: Less than 5 minutes.

Tools: Quiet space.

How: Sit quietly and focus on your breath, a calming image or music.

How did meditation affect your stress levels?

7. Do a quick shoulder roll exercise

Why: Shoulder rolls relieve tension and improve mobility. They are a simple way to relax and warm up.

Time: Less than 5 minutes.

Tools: None.

How: Roll your shoulders forward and backward in a circular motion.

Did the shoulder rolls help release tension in your shoulders?

8. Touch your toes

Why: Touching your toes improves flexibility and relieves lower back tension. It's a simple way to stretch and warm up.

Time: Less than 5 minutes.

Tools: None.

How: Stand and bend forward, reaching for your toes, and hold the stretch.

Did the toe touch stretch help improve your flexibility?

9. Massage your hands or feet

Why: Self-massage can relieve tension and improve circulation. It's a simple way to relax and care for yourself.

Time: 10-20 minutes.

Tools: None.

How: Gently massage your hands or feet, focusing on any tense areas.

Did the massage relieve any tension or discomfort?

10. Do some planks

Why: When you don't have a lot of time to exercise, you can always do some planks. Planking strengthens core muscles, improves posture, and enhances overall stability. It can alleviate lower back pain and build abdominal strength.

Time: 10-20 minutes.

Tools: Exercise mat (optional).

How: Start in a push-up position, then lower onto your forearms. Keep your body in a straight line from head to heels, engaging your core muscles. Hold for 30-60 seconds, gradually increasing duration as you get stronger. If you have lower mobility, you can perform the plank against a wall. Stand next to the wall and hold it as if you were about to do a push-up and then perform the rest of the steps as you would a regular plank.

How does doing plants contribute to your
physical fitness goals?

11. Light a scented candle

Why: Scented candles can create a calming atmosphere and reduce stress. Aromatherapy can promote relaxation.

Time: 10-20 minutes.

Tools: Scented candle, lighter or matches.

How: Light a scented candle and sit quietly, enjoying the aroma.

How did the scent of the candle help you feel more relaxed?

12.   Practice belly breathing

Why: Deep breathing exercises help to calm the mind and the body. Belly breathing especialy reduces stress and lowers blood pressure.

Time: 10-20 minutes.

Tools: Comfortable space, soothing music or sounds of nature (optional).

How: Find a quiet and comfortable place to sit or lie down with quiet music or nature sounds. Place one hand on your belly and the other on your chest. Inhale deeply through your nose, feeling your belly rise, then exhale slowly through your mouth, feeling your belly fall. Repeat for several breaths, focusing on the rhythm of your breath and letting go of tension with each exhale.

How did belly breathing help you feel?

13.   Use essential oils for relaxation

Why: Essential oils can reduce stress and promote relaxation. Aromatherapy can improve mood and well-being.

Time: 10-20 minutes.

Tools: Essential oils, diffuser (optional).

How: Apply a few drops of essential oil to your wrists or use a diffuser.

How did the essential oils help you feel?

14.   Grab some dark grapes

Why: Dark grapes contain resveratrol, an antioxidant with potential anticancer properties. Enjoying them as a snack helps protect cells from damage and supports heart health.

Time: 10-20 minutes.

Tools: Dark grapes.

How: Choose unsweetened grape juice or whole dark grapes as a nutritious snack. Savor the taste and take your time to enjoy them.

Would you consider making dark grapes a regular snack?

15.   Dry brush your skin

Why: Dry brushing your skin is a rejuvenating self-care practice that promotes circulation, exfoliates dead skin cells, and may reduce the appearance of cellulite. It helps invigorate your body and leaves your skin feeling smoother and more vibrant.

Time: 10-20 minutes.

Tools: Dry brush.

How: Before showering, start at your feet and brush toward your heart using gentle, sweeping motions. Use a natural bristle brush and adjust the pressure to your comfort. After dry brushing, shower to rinse off the exfoliated skin cells and follow with moisturizer for extra hydration.

Was dry brushing an enjoyable way to pamper yourself?

16.   Enjoy a piece of chocolate

Why: Indulging in a delicious piece of chocolate as a treat for yourself can be a type of self-care. It boosts your mood, satisfies cravings, and provides a moment of pleasure.

Time: 10-20 minutes.

Tools: Favorite chocolate bar or truffle.

How: Choose a high-quality piece of chocolate that you enjoy. Find a quiet place to sit and savor each bite slowly, letting the rich flavors melt on your tongue. Take this time to fully appreciate the indulgence.

Was chocolate a delightful and satisfying treat?

17.   Practice Kegel Exercises

Why: Kegel exercises strengthen pelvic floor muscles, improving bladder control and sexual function. They can be done discreetly anytime, anywhere.

Time: 10-20 minutes.

Tools: None.

How: Contract and hold your pelvic floor muscles for 5 seconds, then relax for 5 seconds. Repeat 10-15 times in a row. Aim for 3 sets per day.

How did practicing Kegel exercises help your awareness of your pelvic floor muscles?

18. Detangle your hair

Why: Detangling your hair is great for maintaining its health and preventing breakage. It ensures smooth, shiny strands and makes styling easier. It can be a great way to show yourself some love.

Time: 10-20 minutes.

Tools: Detangling brush.

How: Divide your hair into sections. Starting from the ends, gently comb through each section with a detangling brush, working your way up to the roots. Be patient and gentle to avoid damaging your hair.

How did taking the time to detangle your hair impact your hair care routine?

19. Practice breast self-exams

Why: Regular breast self-exams empower you to monitor changes in breast tissue and detect potential abnormalities early.

Time: 10-20 minutes.

Tools: Mirror.

How: Use a mirror to examine your breasts regularly. Get familiar with their texture and appearance to recognize any changes promptly.

How did practicing breast self-exams enhance your sense of proactive health care? How do these exams contribute to your peace of mind?

20. Take a shower to cleanse and relax

Why: A shower cleanses the body, refreshes the mind, and can provide a sense of rejuvenation. It can be the perfect self-care activity to calm and soothe yourself, especially after a difficult day. Warm water helps relax your muscles and relieve tension.

Time: 10-20 minutes.

Tools: Shower gel, loofah or sponge, towel.

How: Step into the shower, adjust the water temperature, lather up with your favorite shower gel, and enjoy the sensation of warm water washing away the day's stresses. Take deep breaths and let go of tension with each rinse.

How did taking a shower work for you? Did you feel more relaxed or refreshed?

21. Eat a healthy snack

Why: Nutritious snacks provide essential vitamins and energy. They can boost your mood and prevent overeating later.

Time: 10-20 minutes.

Tools: Fruits, nuts, yogurt.

How: Choose a healthy snack and eat it mindfully.

How much did the healthy snack improve your energy levels?

22.   Drink a cup of tea

Why: Sometimes, a cup of tea is all you need to help you relax and provide comfort. A good cup of tea calms the mind, hydrates the body, and provides a moment of mindfulness. Different types of teas have different effects on the body. Chamomile tea, for example, is a good bedtime beverage. You can find a tea that suits the purpose you want.

Time: 10-20 minutes.

Tools: Favorite tea blend, teapot or mug, kettle, honey or lemon(optional).

How: Boil water and steep your favorite tea blend in a teapot or mug. Take a moment to inhale the aroma as it brews. Find a cozy spot to sit and slowly sip your tea, savoring the flavors and allowing yourself to unwind.

How did drinking tea change your state?

23.   Practice mindful listening

Why: Mindful listening can improve focus and reduce stress. It promotes a sense of calm and presence.

Time: 10-20 minutes.

Tools: Music or natural sounds.

How: Find a comfortable space where you can listen to music or nature sounds, focusing fully on the experience.

How did mindful listening affect your relaxation levels?

24.   Dance it out

Why: Putting on your favorite dance music and letting loose is a fantastic way to lift your spirits and get your body moving. Having your own personal dance party is self-care too.

Time: 10-20 minutes.

Tools: Favorite dance music.

How: Choose upbeat music that makes you want to dance. Clear a space where you can move freely, and let the music guide your body. Shake off any stress or tension as you dance, and enjoy the freedom of movement.

How did dancing it out make you feel physically and emotionally?

25.   Massage your nails with oil or your favorite hand lotion

Why: Massaging your nails can improve circulation and promote healthier nail growth. It also moisturizes your cuticles and hands, leaving them soft and nourished.

Time: 10-20 minutes.

Tools: Nail oil or hand lotion.

How: Apply a small amount of oil or lotion to your nails and cuticles. Gently massage each nail and cuticle, then rub the lotion into your hands.

How did massaging your nails and hands affect their appearance and how did it make you feel?

26. Use a humidifier

Why: A humidifier can improve air quality and skin hydration. It's especially beneficial in dry environments.

Time: 10-20 minutes.

Tools: Humidifier, water.

How: Set up and turn on a humidifier in your living space.

How much did using the humidifier improve your comfort and skin hydration?

27. Try a guided relaxation video

Why: Guided relaxation can reduce stress and promote a sense of calm. It helps you unwind and recharge.

Time: 10-20 minutes.

Tools: Internet, device to play video.

How: Find a guided relaxation video online and follow along.

In what ways did the guided relaxation help you unwind?

28. Use a heat pack on tense muscles

Why: Heat therapy can relax muscles and relieve pain. It increases blood flow and promotes healing.

Time: 10-20 minutes.

Tools: Heat pack.

How: Apply a heat pack to any tense or sore muscles.

How did the heat pack relieve your muscle tension?

29.   Make and use a DIY face mask

Why: Creating a DIY face mask is a fun and nurturing self-care activity that nourishes your skin and promotes relaxation. It can rejuvenate your complexion and provide a moment of pampering.

Time: 10-20 minutes.

Tools: Ingredients for face mask (e.g., honey, yogurt, oatmeal, avocado).

How: Choose natural ingredients suited to your skin type and mix them into a paste. Apply the mask to your cleansed face, avoiding the eyes. Relax for 10-15 minutes as the mask works its magic. Rinse with warm water and pat dry.

How did making and using the DIY face mask contribute to your sense of well-being and relaxation?

30.   Take time to eat breakfast in the morning

Why: Eating a nutritious breakfast provides essential energy and nutrients to start your day. It can improve concentration, metabolism, and overall health.

Time: 10-20 minutes.

Tools: Healthy breakfast ingredients.

How: Prepare a balanced breakfast with proteins, fruits, and whole grains. Sit down and enjoy your meal without rushing.

How did taking time to eat breakfast affect your energy levels and focus throughout the day?

31.   Wake up at 6 A.M.

Why: Waking up early allows you to start your day peacefully and enjoy the quiet morning hours. It sets a positive tone for the day ahead.

Time: 20-30 minutes.

Tools: Alarm clock.

How: Set your alarm for 6 A.M. and wake up gradually. Take a moment to stretch, sip a glass of water, and step outside to breathe in the fresh morning air. Embrace the slower pace and peaceful atmosphere of the early morning.

How did waking up at 6 A.M. influence your morning routine and overall day?

32.   Give your ears a rest

Why: Taking a break from constant noise can reduce stress and prevent hearing damage. It helps refresh your mind and promotes a sense of calm.

Time: 20-30 minutes.

Tools: Quiet space.

How: Find a quiet place and spend time without any background noise. Turn off all electronic devices and focus on the silence.

How did giving your ears a rest affect your stress levels and sense of calm?

33.   Take a power nap

Why: A short nap can restore alertness, improve mood, and enhance cognitive performance. It helps reduce fatigue and recharge your energy levels.

Time: 20-30 minutes.

Tools: Quiet space, comfortable place to lie down, alarm clock or timer.

How: Find a quiet, comfortable place to lie down. Set an alarm for 15-30 minutes to avoid oversleeping, then close your eyes and rest.

How did taking a power nap affect your energy levels and productivity?

34.   Give yourself a facial

Why: Treating your face with skincare will give you a fresh and glowing complexion. It cleanses pores and improves skin texture.

Time: 20-30 minutes.

Tools: Facial cleanser, exfoliating scrub (optional), face mask, moisturizer.

How: Start by cleansing your face with a gentle cleanser, exfoliate if needed. Apply a face mask suited to your skin type, and finish with moisturizer. Take your time and enjoy the process, massaging the products into your skin.

How was the facial beneficial for your skin?

35.   Go for a walk in the sunshine

Why: Walking in the sunshine boosts your mood and provides essential vitamin D. It helps improve your physical and mental well-being.

Time: 20-30 minutes.

Tools: Comfortable shoes, sunscreen.

How: Find a safe, sunny place to walk. Apply sunscreen and take a walk, enjoying the sunlight and fresh air.

How did walking in the sunshine affect your mood and energy levels?

36.   Foot soak

Why: Soaking your feet can relieve stress, reduce swelling, and improve circulation. It provides a relaxing experience that soothes tired muscles and can improve overall well-being.

Time: 20-30 minutes.

Tools: Basin, warm water, Epsom salt or essential oils, towel.

How: Fill a basin with warm water and add Epsom salt or a few drops of your favorite essential oil. Place your feet in the basin and soak for 15-20 minutes. Dry your feet with a towel and consider applying moisturizer for extra care.

How did enjoying a foot soak affect your stress levels and the comfort of your feet?

37.   Take a warm bath

Why: A warm bath can relax muscles and improve mood. It provides a soothing break from daily stressors.

Time: 20-30 minutes.

Tools: Bath, warm water.

How: Fill your bathtub with warm water and soak for a while.

How did you feel after the bath?

38.   Meal plan for the week

Why: Meal planning helps you stay organized and make healthier food choices throughout the week. It ensures that you have nutritious meals ready, reducing stress and last-minute decisions.

Time: 30-60 minutes.

Tools: Recipes, grocery list, planner.

How: Choose recipes, make a grocery list, and plan your meals for the week.

How did meal planning for the week affect your eating habits and stress levels?

39.   Enjoy a favorite hobby

Why: Engaging in a hobby can provide relaxation and joy. It helps take your mind off stressors and promotes creativity.

Time: 30-60 minutes.

Tools: Hobby-specific tools or materials.

How: Spend time doing a hobby you love, such as knitting, painting, or playing an instrument.

How did engaging in your hobby make you feel?

40. Visit a steam room or sauna

Why: Visiting a sauna or steam room can provide numerous health benefits, including relaxation, improved circulation, and detoxification.

Time: 30-60 minutes (including travel etc).

Tools: Access to a sauna or steam room, towel, water bottle.

How: Find a nearby sauna or steam room. Schedule a visit and bring a towel and water bottle. Spend 15-20 minutes in the sauna or steam room, making sure to stay hydrated.

How did visiting a sauna or steam room affect your stress levels and overall sense of well-being?

41. Schedule a health checkup

Why: Regular health checkups can catch potential issues early and ensure you maintain good health. They provide peace of mind and promote proactive health management.

Time: 1-2 hours.

Tools: Healthcare provider, appointment.

How: Schedule and attend regular screenings recommended for your age and health status. Stay informed about Pap smear intervals and HPV vaccination to reduce cervical cancer risk.

How did scheduling and attending a health checkup impact your sense of health and well-being?

42.   Sleep naked

Why: Sleeping without clothes allows your skin to breathe freely and promotes better circulation. It enhances your overall comfort during sleep.

Time: Overnight.

Tools: Comfortable, breathable sleepwear (optional).

How: Simply remove your clothes before bed. If you must wear something, choose loose, breathable sleepwear.

How did sleeping naked improve your sleep quality or comfort?

43.   Develop a healthy sleep routine

Why: A consistent sleep routine can significantly improve your sleep quality and duration. It helps regulate your body's clock and can improve your overall health and daily functioning.

Time: Overnight.

Tools: Comfortable bedding, quiet environment, alarm clock.

How: Set a regular bedtime and wake-up time, even on weekends. Prepare your bedroom environment to enhance sleep: ensure it is dark, quiet, cool, and comfortable. Avoid stimulants like caffeine and electronics at least an hour before bed. Establish a calming pre-sleep routine such as reading, taking a warm bath, or practicing relaxation exercises.

How did establishing a healthy sleep routine affect your sleep quality and how you feel during the day?

44.   Eat slowly

Why: Eating slowly aids digestion and helps you enjoy your food more. It can prevent overeating and promote a healthier relationship with food.

Time: Ongoing.

Tools: None.

How: Take smaller bites and chew your food thoroughly. Put down your utensils between bites and take a moment to appreciate the taste and texture of each mouthful. Pay attention to your body's signals of hunger and fullness.

How did eating slowly affect your enjoyment of the meal and your fullness level?

45.   Support your oral microbiome

Why: Maintaining a balanced oral microbiome is essential for preventing dental issues and maintaining fresh breath. It also contributes to overall health by reducing harmful bacteria.

Time: Ongoing.

Tools: Probiotic-rich foods, oral probiotics, oral hygiene products.

How: Brush and floss your teeth regularly, use an alcohol-free mouthwash, and incorporate probiotic-rich foods like yogurt into your diet. Consider using oral probiotic lozenges.

How did supporting your oral microbiome impact your oral health? Did you notice any improvements in your oral hygiene?

46.   Support your gut microbiome

Why: A healthy gut microbiome is crucial for digestion, immunity, and overall health. It helps reduce inflammation and improve nutrient absorption.

Time: Ongoing.

Tools: Probiotic and prebiotic-rich foods, supplements.

How: Eat foods rich in probiotics (like yogurt, sauerkraut) and prebiotics (like garlic, onions`, and consider taking supplements if needed.

Did you notice any changes in digestion or energy levels?

CHAPTER 6
SELF-CARE FOR YOUR MIND

The way you think and the things that you fill your mind with greatly influence your psychological well-being. Self-care for your mind is about doing things to keep it sharp and to make sure that its influence on your psychological well-being is the best it can be. Here are some self-care affirmations for your mind:

- I give my mind the care and attention it deserves.
- My brain is amazingly strong, it helps me do incredible things.
- I am not in a hurry when I learn.
- Thank you, brain, for helping me make the best choices today.
- I am smart. I am positive and I am determined to keep growing.

The goal of this chapter is to provide you with activities to engage your intellect and relieve mental stress.

The Activities

47.　Try self-soothing touch

Why: Self-soothing touch, like placing hands on your heart and belly, promotes relaxation and mindfulness, supporting mental self-care through physical and emotional connection.

Time: Less than 5 minutes.

Tools: Hands.

How: Place one hand on your heart and the other on your belly, breathe deeply, and focus on the sensation of touch and breath.

How does self-soothing touch help you center yourself and support your mental calmness?

48.　Pat the inside of your wrist with your other hand

Why: This is a form of EFT tapping that reduces stress hormones and promotes emotional regulation, stress relief, and mental clarity.

Time: Less than 5 minutes.

Tools: Hands.

How: Focus on how you're feeling right now. Close your eyes, pat your wrist, and breathe slowly.

How did practicing tapping improve your mental state? Would you explore EFT more?

49. Progressive muscle relaxation

Why: Purposefully tensing and then relaxing muscle groups helps reduce anxiety and promote mental calmness.

Time: Less than 5 minutes.

Tools: Quiet space, relaxation scripts or soothing sounds.

How: Sit or lie quietly. Starting with your head and moving down to your toes, tense and relax different muscle groups. Focus on deep breathing and releasing tension as you move your attention down your body.

How does relaxation training help you relax?

50. Watch an ASMR video

Why: Promote relaxation, stress relief, and sensory comfort by watching ASMR (Autonomous Sensory Meridian Response) videos.

Time: Less than 5 minutes.

Tools: ASMR videos, headphones.

How: Find ASMR videos that cater to your preferences, such as whispering, tapping, or soothing sounds. Use headphones for an immersive experience. Focus on the sensory stimuli and allow yourself to unwind and relax deeply.

How did watching ASMR videos promote relaxation and stress relief for you?

51.   Visualize success

Why: Creating a mental blueprint of what success looks and feels like can improve focus, boost self-esteem, and make achieving goals feel more attainable. Athletes and successful business professionals often use this to prepare for upcoming challenges.

Time: Less than 5 minutes.

Tools: Quiet space.

How: Close your eyes and visualize yourself successfully completing a task you're anxious about.

How did visualizing success change your approach to the task?

52.   Affirmation practice

Why: Daily affirmations reinforce positive thinking, boost self-esteem, and can rewire thought patterns toward more optimistic and productive attitudes.

Time: Less than 5 minutes.

Tools: Mirror, Affirmations from the start of this chapter.

How: Each morning or evening, stand in front of a mirror, select one or two affirmations from your list, and confidently speak them out loud to yourself.

How do you feel after repeating your affirmations, and how do they influence your mindset?

53.   Read a poem

Why: Reading poetry can enrich language skills, evoke emotions, and stimulate reflective thinking, offering a unique perspective on language and life.

Time: Less than 5 minutes.

Tools: Book or online.

How: Read a short poem and reflect on its imagery and themes.

What emotions or thoughts did the poem evoke?

54.   Practice using your non-dominant hand

Why: This is called becoming ambidextrous, and it challenges and strengthens your brain by stimulating the development of new neural pathways.

Time: 5-10 minutes.

Tools: Common tools like a toothbrush, pen, computer mouse.

How: Use your non-dominant hand for daily tasks like eating, writing, or brushing your teeth.

How challenging was it to get tasks done with your non-dominant hand?

55. Mind enhancing puzzle

Why: Regularly solving puzzles enhances cognitive function, improves problem-solving skills, and can help maintain mental agility as you age. This could be a crossword, cryptogram, word search, and similar.

Time: 5-10 minutes.

Tools: Puzzle book, app, pen or similar.

How: Solve a quick puzzle to engage your mind and focus.

How did completing the puzzle make you feel mentally?

56. Pop bubble wrap

Why: Popping bubble wrap is a sensory activity that can reduce stress and provide a momentary distraction from cognitive overload.

Time: 5-10 minutes.

Tools: Bubble wrap.

How: Use a piece of bubble wrap and pop the bubbles, focusing on the sensation and sound.

How did popping bubble wrap affect your stress levels and concentration?

57. Sing your favorite song

Why: Singing can boost mental health and improve mood. It's a joyful expression that engages both emotional and cognitive centers. Even if you think you don't have a great voice, sing anyway!

Time: 5-10 minutes.

Tools: Music player, lyrics if needed.

How: Sing along to your favorite song, using music or going acapella.

How did singing your favorite song uplift your spirits and engage your memory?

58. Count backwards from 100

Why: Counting backwards improves concentration and cognitive control. It's a simple exercise to focus the mind and reduce distractions.

Time: 5-10 minutes.

Tools: None.

How: Quietly count backwards from 100 to 1, focusing solely on the numbers.

How did counting backwards challenge your concentration and mental control?

59.   Read fiction for ten minutes

Why: Reading fiction provides an escape and stimulates the imagination. Your mind will thank you for it.

Time: 10-20 minutes.

Tools: A great fiction book.

How: Choose a fiction book that interests you. Find a quiet, comfortable spot and allow yourself to get lost in the narrative.

How did reading fiction enhance your relaxation or creativity?

60.   Catch up on your favorite blog

Why: Reading your favorite blog updates you on topics of interest and gives valuable insights, entertainment, and a break from the demands of daily tasks.

Time: 10-20 minutes.

Tools: Internet access, favorite blog.

How: Visit your preferred blog platform and explore recent posts. Read posts that inspire or inform you, and consider sharing your thoughts in the comments.

How did catching up on your favorite blog content enrich your knowledge or spark your curiosity?

61.   Color with crayons

Why: Adult coloring can help you relax and the moment. It is also a great way to let yourself be creative.

Time: 10-20 minutes.

Tools: Coloring book, crayons or colored pens or pencils.

How: Choose a coloring book theme that appeals to you. Find a quiet space, select colors mindfully, and immerse yourself in coloring intricate designs.

How coloring help you unwind or reduce stress?

62.   Meditate for 10 minutes

Why: Research shows that practicing meditation, even if you've never done it before, helps to reduce stress, increase focus, and promote a sense of peace and well-being.

Time: 10-20 minutes.

Tools: Quiet space, meditation app or timer.

How: Find a comfortable, quiet place to sit. Focus on your breath or use a guided meditation app.

How did meditation affect your focus and emotional state throughout the day?

63.   Sing to solve problems

Why: Singing stimulates creativity and pattern recognition in the brain, promoting emotional expression and cognitive processing.

Time: 10-20 minutes.

Tools: Voice, favorite songs.

How: Sing about your worries or problems to a familiar tune. Focus on expression and melody.

What new perspectives or possible solutions emerged from singing your problems?

64.   Talk back to your inner critic

Why: Addressing and talking back to your inner critic means recognizing and challenging your negative self-talk, which can boost self-esteem and promote a healthier, more balanced self-perception.

Time: 10-20 minutes.

Tools: Pen and paper or notebook.

How: When your inner critic speaks, counter it by writing a list of things you appreciate about yourself. Keep it handy to refer to during moments of self-doubt. Add to the list often.

How did appreciating yourself change your perspective of yourself?

65. Fix a small annoyance at home that's been nagging you

Why: Taking care of a small annoyance sends a message to your brain that you have the inner resources to fix what's needed. This gives you a sense of personal power and accomplishment.

Time: 10-20 minutes.

Tools: Basic tools or replacement parts.

How: Identify and fix a small issue at home that bothers you, such as sewing on a lost button, fixing a stuck drawer, or replacing a burnt-out light bulb.

How did fixing this annoyance improve your living space or mood?

66. Watch a TED Talk

Why: TED Talks can inspire, educate, and provide insights from experts in various fields, all designed to spark curiosity and encourage personal and professional growth.

Time: 10-20 minutes.

Tools: Internet access, phone or computer.

How: Choose a TED Talk that interests you or is about a skill you want to develop.

What new ideas or insights did you gain from the TED Talk?

67. Identify bird species

Why: Enhances observational skills, increases knowledge of local wildlife, and fosters a deeper appreciation for biodiversity and environmental conservation.

Time: 10-20 minutes.

Tools: Book or bird app.

How: Observe birds in your area and try to identify their species using a guidebook or app.

How did focusing on nature affect your state of mind?

68. Memorize a phone number

Why: Improves cognitive flexibility and memory retention. Regular mental exercises like memorization can strengthen neural connections.

Time: 10-20 minutes.

Tools: Phone number, notepad.

How: Choose a phone number you often use but haven't memorized. Write it down and practice recalling it several times throughout the day.

How did the process of memorizing a phone number challenge your memory skills?

69. Switch hands

Why: Using your non-dominant hand can improve brain function and neural connections. It challenges your brain in new ways.

Time: 10-20 minutes.

Tools: Any activity that involves hand usage.

How: Try using your non-dominant hand for daily activities like brushing your teeth or writing.

How did using your non-dominant hand affect your manual dexterity and brain activity?

70. Do a Sudoku puzzle

Why: Doing a Sudoku puzzle helps improve your problem-solving skills and keeps your mind sharp.

Time: 10-20 minutes.

Tools: A Sudoku puzzle (either on paper or digital).

How: Set aside some time to work on a Sudoku puzzle, focusing on filling in the grid with numbers according to the game's rules, without guessing.

Reflection: How did solving the Sudoku puzzle challenge your problem-solving skills?

71. Practice balancing

Why: Balancing exercises engage both the body and mind, improving physical coordination and mental focus.

Time: 10-20 minutes.

Tools: Flat, stable surface.

How: Stand on one foot and maintain balance as long as you can, then switch feet.

How did practicing balancing affect your physical coordination and mental focus?

72. Plan a daydream

Why: Allowing yourself to daydream can boost creativity, problem-solving skills, and provide mental relaxation.

Time: 10-20 minutes.

Tools: Quiet space.

How: Find a quiet place to sit comfortably, let your mind wander, and consciously choose a pleasant scenario to imagine.

How did planning a daydream affect your creativity and wellbeing?

73.   Start learning a new language

Why: Learning a new language take involves regular, structured practice sessions that improve your cognitive skills, enhance memory, increase mental flexibility, and broaden your cultural understanding.

Time: 20-30 minutes.

Tools: Language learning app or course, study materials.

How: Choose a language that interests you or aligns with your personal or work goals. Practice consistently to improve your fluency and understanding.

How does learning a new language improve your communication skills and open new opportunities for learning?

74.   Arrange a bookshelf thematically

Why: Facilitates easier access and retrieval of books, stimulates cognitive organization skills, and can also rejuvenate your interest in reading.

Time: 20-30 minutes.

Tools: Bookshelf, books.

How: Organize your books by theme, color, or author, making decisions on grouping.

How did organizing affect your thought process?

75. Learn to juggle

Why: Improves hand-eye coordination, concentration, and neural connectivity, while also serving as a fun and challenging physical activity.

Time: 20-30 minutes.

Tools: 3 small balls or objects.

How: Practice juggling with three balls, starting with two in one hand and one in the other.

How did learning to juggle challenge your coordination?

76. Learn five new words

Why: Expanding vocabulary can enhance language skills and cognitive function. It also aids in creative and critical thinking.

Time: 20-30 minutes.

Tools: Dictionary, notebook.

How: Pick up a dictionary or use a language app to learn five new words and their meanings. Try to use them in sentences throughout the day.

How did learning new words expand your vocabulary and affect your language use?

77. Map out a new route

Why: Navigating a new route can enhance spatial awareness and problem-solving skills. It encourages mental mapping and adaptability.

Time: 20-30 minutes.

Tools: Map, GPS.

How: Plan a new route for a familiar destination and follow it without GPS help once you understand the path.

How did mapping out and following a new route challenge your navigation skills?

78. Look at old photos

Why: Looking at old photos can stimulate memories and emotional processing, enhancing mental connections and mood.

Time: 20-30 minutes.

Tools: Photo albums or digital photos.

How: Spend time going through old photos, recalling the events and people in them.

How did revisiting old photos affect your mood and memory recall?

79.   Solve a crossword puzzle

Why: Solving crossword puzzles can improve vocabulary, enhance problem-solving skills, and provide mental stimulation. It's a fun way to challenge your cognitive abilities and improve focus.

Time: 20-30 minutes.

Tools: Crossword puzzle (newspaper, book, or online app).

How: Choose a crossword puzzle from a newspaper, book, or an online app. Spend time solving it, focusing on understanding the clues and finding the correct words.

How did solving a crossword puzzle challenge your cognitive skills and affect your ability to focus?

80.   Watch a sunrise or sunset

Why: Watching a sunrise or sunset can provide mental relaxation and inspiration. It encourages mindfulness and a connection with nature.

Time: 20-30 minutes.

Tools: None, just a good viewing spot.

How: Find a spot where you can clearly see the horizon and watch the sunrise or sunset. Reflect on the experience.

How did watching a sunrise or sunset affect your feelings of peace and mindfulness?

81.   List future learning goals

Why: Setting learning goals can motivate personal development and intellectual growth. It helps organize and prioritize learning endeavors.

Time: 20-30 minutes.

Tools: Notebook, pen.

How: Write down a list of topics or skills you want to learn about in the future.

How did setting learning goals affect your motivation and plans for personal development?

82.   Declutter one of your social media accounts

Why: This can help to reduce digital noise and distractions, reduce overwhelm and align your feed more closely with your values and interests. This could make social media more meaningful and uplifting.

Time: 30-60 minutes.

Tools: Computer or smartphone.

How: Start with one social media account and unfollow accounts that no longer serve you. Delete old messages. Unfollow inactive accounts.

How did cleaning up your digital space improve your productivity?

83.   Create a personal mission statement

Why: A personal mission statement helps you reflect on, clarify and understand your core values passions and goals. This helps you decide how you want to impact the world around you and gives you a focused framework for decision-making and personal growth.

Time: 30-60 minutes.

Tools: Pen and paper or digital notepad.

How: Start by listing your core values, guiding principles, and long-term impact you want to make. Write this as a simple statement in clear, affirmative language that inspires and motivates you. Revisit and update your mission statement regularly.

How does having a clear mission statement impact your daily choices?

84.   Play a video game

Why: Playing different video games stimulates cognitive functions, mental agility and improves problem-solving skills.

Time: 30-60 minutes.

Tools: Gaming console or computer.

How: Play a variety of video games that challenge different aspects of cognition including memory, problem-solving and pattern recognition.

How challenged did you feel by the video game?

85.   Go star gazing

Why: Taking time to be outside at night helps you relax, wonder at, and appreciate nature by watching clouds or stars in the night sky.

Time: 30-60 minutes.

Tools: Open outdoor space, stargazing apps or guides.

How: Choose a clear evening and find a location away from city lights for optimal viewing of clouds or stars. Use stargazing apps or guides to identify constellations, planets, or celestial events. Take time to observe the beauty of the sky and contemplate the vastness of the universe.

How did star gazing enhance your sense of wonder and appreciation for nature? Did it provide you with moments of tranquility and reflection?

86.   Listen to a podcast on a new topic

Why: Listening to podcasts on new topics can broaden knowledge and stimulate interest in different subjects. It promotes continuous learning.

Time: 30-60 minutes.

Tools: Podcast app, headphones.

How: Find a podcast on a topic you know little about and listen to an episode. Reflect on what you learned.

How did listening to a new topic broaden your perspectives or interests?

87.   Try laughter yoga

Why: Laughter Yoga combines laughter exercises with yoga breathing techniques, which can reduce stress, improve mood, and enhance overall mental and physical health. Engaging in this activity promotes relaxation and boosts the immune system while fostering a sense of joy and social connection.

Time: 30-60 minutes.

Tools: Comfortable clothing, a Laughter Yoga group or online video.

How: Find a Laughter Yoga class in your area or look up a guided Laughter Yoga session online. Wear comfortable clothing and follow the instructor's lead, which typically involves a series of laughter exercises combined with deep yogic breathing. Embrace the process openly. even if the laughter is forced initially, as it often leads to genuine laughter.

How did participating in Laughter Yoga affect your mood and stress levels?

88.   Try a new recipe

Why: Trying a new recipe can stimulate creativity and improve cognitive sequencing and planning skills.

Time: 1-2 hours.

Tools: Recipe, ingredients, kitchen tools.

How: Choose a recipe you've never made before and follow the steps to prepare the dish.

How did trying a new recipe challenge your cooking skills and ability to follow complex instructions?

89.   Attend a trivia night

Why: Promote social engagement, teamwork, and mental agility by participating in trivia nights or quiz competitions.

Time: 1-2 hours.

Tools: Trivia night venue, friends or team.

How: Find local venues or virtual platforms that host trivia nights or quiz events. Form a team with friends or join as an individual to test your knowledge across different topics.

How did attending a trivia night promote social engagement and mental stimulation?

90.   Learn a new board game

Why: Learning a new board game introduces mental stimulation. It challenges your brain to think in new dimensions and create neural pathways keeping it young and agile.

Time: 1-2 hours.

Tools: Board game.

How: Gather friends or family if you can or look for online tutorials or virtual games. Embrace the challenge of learning new rules and enjoy the thinking required to play.

How did learning a new board game bring enjoyment or intellectual satisfaction?

91. Protein day challenge

Why: Eating protein-rich foods like fish, chicken, turkey, and beans have high levels of essential amino acids and nutrients that support brain health. Adding them to your daily diet can enhance cognitive functions such as focus, memory, and mental energy.

Time: One day.

Tools: Meal plan for the day.

How: Create a meal plan for one day that includes fish, chicken, turkey, eggs, or beans in each meal. Eat proteins you prefer. Prepare ahead if needed.

What differences did you notice in how you felt mentally and physically during the challenge compared to a typical day?

92. Disconnect from technology and media for a day

Why: Taking a break from technology and media helps alleviate stress, reduces information overload, and improves focus and mental well-being by encouraging activities that don't involve screens. It can give your mind a reset and gain a fresh perspective.

Time: One day.

Tools: Timer or reminder.

How: Turn off your phone, avoid social media, and limit screen time to essential tasks only. Spend the day engaging in offline activities like reading, walking, or spending time with loved ones.

How did disconnecting from technology impact your day?

CHAPTER 7
SELF-CARE FOR YOUR FEELINGS

Most of us are familiar with soothing and caring for other people's feelings especially when they are going through a difficult time. This chapter will help you become your own friend and take care of your feelings as well. In a sense, the activities in this chapter will help you regulate your emotions. Some of them can be used at the moment when your emotions are running high while others are for general emotional maintenance. To get you started, here are some self-care affirmations for your feelings:

- My feelings deserve the best consideration and care.
- I give myself permission to feel as I do.
- I care for my feelings with love and compassion, as I do for my child or my best friend.
- Taking care of my feelings is my responsibility.
- When I am kind to myself, it's easy to be kind to others.

In this chapter, you will find activities to better manage your emotions, improve emotional resilience and navigate your feelings effectively.

The Activities

93.   Write down three things you're grateful for

Why: Reflecting on specific moments of gratitude can boost your mood and reduce stress. It helps you focus on the positive aspects of your day and promotes a habit of mindfulness.

Time: Less than 5 minutes.

Tools: Quiet space, journal or notepad.

How: Find a quiet place and sit comfortably. Think about three specific things you're grateful for today. Write them down in your journal, describing why you appreciate them and how they made you feel.

How did reflecting on these three things affect your mood and perspective on your day?

94.   Write and repeat positive affirmations

Why: Writing and repeating positive affirmations can boost self-esteem and confidence. It helps reinforce a positive mindset and encourages self-belief.

Time: Less than 5 minutes.

Tools: Paper, pen or digital device.

How: Write down a list of positive affirmations that resonate with you, such as "I am capable," "I am deserving of happiness," or "I am strong." Repeat them to yourself daily, preferably in front of a mirror.

How did writing and repeating positive affirmations impact your self-esteem and mindset?

95.   Deep breathing exercise

Why: Deep breathing can reduce stress and promote relaxation. It helps calm the mind and improve focus by increasing oxygen flow.

Time: Less than 5 minutes.

Tools: None.

How: Sit comfortably in a quiet place. Close your eyes and take a deep breath in through your nose, hold it for a few seconds, and then slowly exhale through your mouth. Repeat this cycle for several minutes, focusing on your breath.

How did the deep breathing exercise affect your stress levels and mental clarity?

96.   Squeeze a stress ball

Why: Using a stress ball can help release physical tension and reduce stress. It provides a simple way to keep your hands busy and channel nervous energy.

Time: Less than 5 minutes.

Tools: Stress ball.

How: Hold a stress ball in one hand and squeeze it as hard as you can, then release. Repeat this process several times, focusing on the sensation and how it relieves tension. Switch hands and repeat.

How did using a stress ball affect your physical tension and stress levels?

97.   Take a self-compassion break

Why: Taking a self-compassion break can reduce stress and improve emotional well-being. It helps you treat yourself with kindness and understanding during difficult moments.

Time: Less than 5 minutes.

Tools: A quiet place.

How: Find a quiet place and sit comfortably. Close your eyes and take a few deep breaths. Silently offer yourself words of comfort and kindness, such as "It's okay to feel this way" or "I am doing my best." Reflect on how you would support a friend in a similar situation and extend that same compassion to yourself.

How did taking a self-compassion break affect your stress levels and emotional well-being?

98.   Take a five-minute dance break

Why: Dancing can boost your mood, increase energy levels, and reduce stress. It provides a fun and active way to take a break from work.

Time: Less than 5 minutes.

Tools: Music player or streaming service.

How: Put on an upbeat song and dance around for a few minutes. Focus on moving your body and having fun.

How did taking a dance break affect your energy levels and mood?

99. Track your mood daily

Why: Keeping a mood tracker can help you identify patterns and triggers in your emotional well-being. It promotes self-awareness and can guide you in managing your emotions.

Time: Less than 5 minutes.

Tools: Mood tracker (printable or app).

How: At the end of each day, record your mood and any notable events or feelings. Reflect on any patterns or triggers you notice over time.

How did tracking your mood daily affect your awareness of your emotions and their triggers?

100. Feel what you're feeling for 90 seconds

Why: Research has shown that our bodies process any emotion in 90 seconds, if we allow it and don't suppress it. Any feeling will pass In 90 seconds.

Time: Less than 5 minutes.

Tools: Timer or clock.

How: Find a quiet space and set a timer for 90 seconds. Close your eyes and focus on your current emotion, whether it's happiness, sadness, anger, or anxiety. Allow yourself to fully feel the emotion without judgment, noticing any physical sensations and thoughts that arise. Breathe deeply and let the emotion flow through you.

How did allowing yourself to fully feel your emotions for 90 seconds affect your emotional state and overall well-being?

101. Visualize a glass wall

Why: Visualizing a glass wall can help you set emotional boundaries, protect your energy, and maintain focus. It promotes a sense of safety and emotional clarity.

Time: Less than 5 minutes.

Tools: Visualization.

How: Visualize a clear glass wall between you and anything that causes stress or discomfort, allowing you to see it without being affected.

How did visualizing a glass wall affect your sense of emotional safety and clarity?

102. Stop apologizing for everything

Why: Research shows that women tend to apologize even when they have done nothing wrong, trying to keep the peace. Peace is good and necessary, but it must never come at your expense. Apologizing when you have done nothing wrong is self-rejection. You deserve to take up space.

Time: Less than 5 minutes.

Tools: Self-compassion, assertiveness.

How: Notice moments when you apologize unnecessarily, especially for expressing emotions like sadness or frustration. Remind yourself that your feelings are valid and worthy of acknowledgment.

How did stopping unnecessary apologies enhance your sense of self-worth and self-acceptance?

103.   List five things you love about your life

Why: Cultivate gratitude and appreciation by identifying and acknowledging positive aspects of your life.

Time: Less than 5 minutes.

Tools: Pen and paper, or digital notepad.

How: Reflect on different areas of your life such as relationships, work, hobbies, and personal achievements. Write down five specific things that bring you joy, fulfillment, or satisfaction. Focus on moments, experiences, or people that contribute positively to your overall well-being.

How did listing things you love about your life enhance your appreciation and positivity?

104.   Use the havening touch

Why: Havening touch is an emotional regulation technique that calms the nervous system, promoting stress reduction and emotional resilience.

Time: 5-10 minutes.

Tools: Hands.

How: Stroke your arms, face, or hands gently while focusing on calming thoughts or memories.

Did using the havening touch help you calm down?

105. Countdown to calmness

Why: Counting down grounds and centers your emotions by helping you to be mindful.

Time: 5-10 minutes.

Tools: Quiet space.

How: Engage your senses by observing and naming things around you in decreasing numbers, focusing on the present moment. Name 5 things you can see, 4 things you can touch, 3 things you can hear, 2 things you can smell and 1 thing you can taste.

How did this exercise help you to calm down?

106. Listen to your favorite calming music

Why: Listening to music can elevate your mood, reduce stress, and promote relaxation. It helps you connect with your emotions and find comfort in soothing sounds.

Time: 10-20 minutes.

Tools: Music player or streaming service, headphones.

How: Choose a playlist of your favorite calming or uplifting songs. Find a quiet space, put on your headphones, and immerse yourself in the music, allowing yourself to feel the emotions it evokes.

What did you think and feel when listening to your favorite calming music?

107. Have an emotional check-in with a friend

Why: Regularly checking in with a friend can provide emotional support and strengthen your relationship. It helps you process your feelings and feel understood.

Time: 10-20 minutes.

Tools: Phone or video call.

How: Schedule a time to talk with a friend. Share how you're feeling and listen to their experiences. Offer support and empathy to each other.

How did the emotional check-in with your friend affect your mood and sense of connection?

108. Reflect on your personal achievements

Why: Reflecting on your achievements can boost self-esteem and motivation. It helps you recognize your progress and feel proud of your accomplishments.

Time: 10-20 minutes.

Tools: Quiet space, journal or notepad.

How: Find a quiet place to sit comfortably. Write down your recent achievements, big or small, and reflect on the effort and skills that went into them.

How did reflecting on your personal achievements impact your self-esteem and motivation?

109. Create a DIY aromatherapy experience

Why: Aromatherapy can reduce stress, improve mood, and promote relaxation. Using scents that you find calming can create a soothing environment for emotional well-being.

Time: 10-20 minutes.

Tools: Essential oils, diffuser or spray bottle, or natural items like citrus peels and herbs.

How: Choose an essential oil like lavender, eucalyptus, or citrus. Use a diffuser or spray bottle to disperse the scent in your workspace or home. Or use natural items like citrus peels and herbs in a bowl of hot water to release their aroma.

How did the aromatherapy experience affect your mood and stress levels?

110. Practice a body scan meditation

Why: A body scan meditation can help you relax and become more aware of physical sensations. It promotes mindfulness and reduces tension.

Time: 10-20 minutes.

Tools: Quiet space.

How: Sit or lie down in a comfortable position. Close your eyes and slowly focus on each part of your body from head to toe, noticing any sensations without judgment.

How did practicing a body scan meditation affect your physical comfort and mindfulness?

95

111. Try a 10-minute yoga routine, on a mat or on a chair

Why: Yoga can improve flexibility, reduce stress, and enhance overall well-being. It combines physical movement with mindfulness, promoting both physical and emotional health.

Time: 10-20 minutes.

Tools: Yoga mat or chair, yoga video or app.

How: Find a beginner-friendly 10-minute yoga routine online or through a yoga app. Follow along, focusing on your breath and how your body feels in each pose.

How did practicing yoga for 10 minutes affect your physical comfort and emotional well-being?

112. Hand and arm exercises

Why: These exercises can improve circulation, reduce tension, and promote relaxation. They are accessible for individuals with limited mobility and can be done anywhere.

Time: 10-20 minutes.

Tools: Comfortable chair.

How: Sit comfortably and perform exercises such as wrist circles, finger stretches, and arm lifts. Focus on slow, controlled movements and your breath.

How did performing hand and arm exercises affect your physical comfort and relaxation?

113. Visualize your safe place

Why: Visualizing a safe place can reduce anxiety and create a sense of calm. It helps you mentally escape to a comforting environment.

Time: 10-20 minutes.

Tools: Quiet space.

How: Find a quiet place to sit comfortably. Close your eyes and imagine a place where you feel completely safe and relaxed. Focus on the details and sensations of this place.

How did visualizing your safe place affect your anxiety and sense of calm?

114. Draw your feelings

Why: Expressing emotions through drawing can help you process and understand your feelings. It provides a creative outlet and promotes emotional awareness.

Time: 10-20 minutes.

Tools: Paper, colored pencils or markers.

How: Find a quiet place to sit comfortably. Take a few moments to reflect on your current emotions. Then, draw whatever comes to mind, using colors and shapes to represent how you feel.

How did drawing your feelings help you understand and process your emotions?

115. Write a self-compassionate letter to yourself

Why: Writing a letter to yourself can help you develop self-compassion and understanding. It helps you offer kindness and support to yourself during challenging times.

Time: 10-20 minutes.

Tools: Quiet space, paper, pen.

How: Find a quiet place to sit comfortably. Write a letter to yourself as if you were writing to a dear friend, offering words of kindness, understanding, and encouragement. Reflect on your struggles and how you are trying your best.

How did writing a self-compassionate letter affect your feelings of self-kindness and emotional support?

116. Forgive yourself for something from your past

Why: Promote self-healing and emotional growth by practicing self-forgiveness for past mistakes or regrets.

Time: 10-20 minutes.

Tools: Reflection, self-compassion.

How: Reflect on a specific event or decision from your past that still weighs on your mind. Acknowledge any guilt or shame associated with it, and practice self-compassion. Remind yourself that mistakes are a part of growth. Write a forgiveness letter to yourself, expressing understanding and acceptance.

How did forgiving yourself for something from your past promote self-healing and growth?

117. Write down three self-love prompts in your journal

Why: Enhance self-awareness and self-compassion by creating positive affirmations and reflections in your journal.

Time: 10-20 minutes.

Tools: Journal, pen.

How: Set aside quiet time to reflect on aspects of yourself that you appreciate and value. Write down prompts such as "What am I grateful for today?", "What makes me unique?", or "How can I be kinder to myself?". Respond to these prompts with honesty and kindness, acknowledging your strengths and achievements.

How did writing self-love prompts in your journal enhance your self-awareness and positivity?

118. Identify things/ experiences/people that shame you

Why: Recognizing sources of shame allows you to address and release their hold on your self-esteem. Your existence does not need to feel like an apology.

Time: 10-20 minutes.

Tools: Self-reflection.

How: Reflect on situations, experiences, or people that trigger feelings of shame. Journal or discuss with a trusted person.

How did identifying and acknowledging sources of shame impact your self-perception and emotional well-being?

119. Dress up for no reason sometimes

Why: Elevate your mood and self-confidence by dressing up in outfits that make you feel good and reflect your personal style.

Time: 10-20 minutes.

Tools: Favorite outfits, accessories.

How: Choose clothing and accessories that make you feel confident and comfortable. Experiment with colors and styles that uplift your mood. Take time to groom and style yourself in a way that boosts your self-esteem and positive energy.

How did dressing up positively impact your mood and self-perception?

120. Perform a simple act of kindness

Why: An act of kindness can boost your mood, improve your emotional well-being, and strengthen social bonds, and build connections and empathy toward others.

Time: 10-20 minutes.

Tools: None or minimal, depending on the act (e.g., pen and paper for a note, small purchase for a gift).

How: Choose a simple act of kindness that you can do easily, like sending an encouraging text message, paying for someone's coffee, or helping someone carry groceries. Do it with sincerity and without expecting anything in return.

How did performing a simple act of kindness affect your mood and perception of social connections?

121. Schedule a virtual coffee date with a friend

Why: Connecting with friends, even virtually, can boost your mood and provide emotional support. It helps maintain social bonds and reduces feelings of isolation.

Time: 20-30 minutes.

Tools: Computer or smartphone, video conferencing app.

How: Schedule a time to have a virtual coffee date with a friend using a video conferencing app. Prepare your favorite drink and chat about your day, share stories, and catch up.

How did having a virtual coffee date with a friend affect your mood and sense of connection?

122. Write a gratitude letter to someone special

Why: Writing a gratitude letter can improve your mood and strengthen relationships. It helps you focus on the positive impact others have on your life and express appreciation.

Time: 20-30 minutes.

Tools: Paper and pen or computer.

How: Think of someone you are grateful for and write a letter to them, detailing why you appreciate them and specific ways they have positively impacted your life. If possible, deliver the letter in person or send it to them.

How did writing and sending a gratitude letter affect your emotions and your relationship with the recipient?

123. Practice Loving-Kindness Meditation

Why: Practicing Loving-Kindness Meditation can develop and grow feelings of compassion and connection, reducing negative emotions and enhancing emotional well-being. It helps you develop a more positive and caring attitude toward yourself and others.

Time: 20-30 minutes.

Tools: Quiet space, comfortable seating.

How: Find a quiet space where you can sit comfortably. Close your eyes and take a few deep breaths to relax. Silently repeat phrases such as "May I be happy, may I be healthy, may I be safe, may I live with ease," directing these wishes first to yourself, then to someone you love, then to a neutral person, and finally to someone with whom you have difficulties.

How did practicing loving-kindness meditation affect your feelings toward yourself and others?

124. Read a chapter from a personal development book

Why: Reading personal development books can provide new insights, inspire growth, and improve motivation. It helps you learn new strategies for self-improvement and well-being.

Time: 20-30 minutes.

Tools: Personal development book or e-book.

How: Choose a personal development book that interests you and read a chapter. Reflect on the key takeaways and how you can apply them to your life.

How did reading a chapter from a personal development book influence your motivation and outlook on self-improvement?

125.   Listen to a sound bath recording

Why: Sound baths use soothing sounds to promote relaxation and reduce stress. They can help you unwind and create a calming atmosphere.

Time: 20-30 minutes.

Tools: Headphones, sound bath recording or app.

How: Find a sound bath recording or app and listen with headphones in a quiet space. Focus on the different tones and vibrations to enhance relaxation.

How did listening to a sound bath affect your stress levels and overall sense of relaxation?

126.   Go for a nature walk

Why: Walking in nature can reduce stress and improve mood by connecting you with the natural environment. It promotes physical activity and mindfulness.

Time: 20-30 minutes.

Tools: Comfortable shoes, outdoor space.

How: Find a nearby park, trail, or any natural setting. Walk at a comfortable pace, focusing on the sights, sounds, and smells around you. Take deep breaths and enjoy the natural surroundings.

How did walking in nature affect your mood and stress levels?

127. Create an emotion-themed playlist

Why: Music can evoke and enhance specific emotions. Creating a playlist based on a particular mood can help you process and embrace your feelings.

Time: 20-30 minutes.

Tools: Music player or streaming service.

How: Choose a theme for your playlist, such as "Happy," "Calm," or "Motivated." Select songs that fit this theme and create a playlist. Use it during activities like a dance break or relaxation time.

How did listening to your emotion-themed playlist affect your mood and emotional processing?

128. Use creative writing prompts to explore emotions

Why: Creative writing can provide a therapeutic outlet for expressing emotions. It helps you explore your feelings in a structured yet imaginative way.

Time: 20-30 minutes.

Tools: Creative writing prompts, paper, pen or computer.

How: Find a list of creative writing prompts that focus on emotions. Choose a prompt and write a short story, poem, or personal reflection based on it.

How did using creative writing prompts help you express and understand your emotions?

129. Buy yourself fresh flowers

Why: Treating yourself to fresh flowers nurtures joy and appreciation for simple pleasures.

Time: 20-30 minutes.

Tools: Local flower shop, online delivery.

How: Visit a local florist or order flowers online that bring you joy. Arrange them in a vase and display them in a place where you spend time.

How did buying yourself fresh flowers uplift your mood and enhance your environment?

130. Nurture your inner child

Why: Connecting with your inner child can help you heal past emotional wounds and foster self-compassion. It promotes emotional well-being and self-acceptance.

Time: 20-30 minutes.

Tools: Quiet space, journal, childhood photos (optional).

How: Find a quiet place and reflect on a happy childhood memory. Write about it in a journal, including how it made you feel. If possible, look at old photos to enhance the experience.

How did nurturing your inner child affect your emotional well-being and self-compassion?

131. Create a comfort box

Why: A comfort box filled with items that bring you joy and comfort can provide immediate relief during stressful times. It serves as a personalized self-care toolkit.

Time: 20-30 minutes.

Tools: A box, comforting items (e.g., photos, snacks, scented candles).

How: Choose a box and fill it with items that make you feel happy and relaxed, such as favorite snacks, photos, a cozy blanket, or a scented candle. Keep this box handy for times when you need a mood boost.

How did creating and using a comfort box affect your ability to manage stress and improve your mood?

132. Volunteer for an online cause

Why: Volunteering online can give you a sense of purpose and connection while helping others. It can boost your mood and provide a fulfilling break from your routine.

Time: 30-60 minutes.

Tools: Computer, internet access.

How: Find a cause or organization you care about and sign up for online volunteering opportunities. This could include tasks like mentoring, writing, or graphic design.

How did volunteering online impact your sense of purpose and emotional well-being?

133. Create or buy an emotion wheel picture

Why: An emotion wheel helps you identify your emotions better. It helps you understand your emotions by showing how they relate to one another, and improve the way you talk about emotional nuances.

Time: 30-60 minutes.

Tools: Paper, pen, coloring tools, book about emotions, or buy online.

How: You can create your own emotion wheel by drawing a large circle divided into sections, each labeled with different emotions. Or buy an emotion wheel online and print it. Use the wheel daily or during emotional moments to identify and name your feelings.

How did using the emotion wheel affect your ability to identify and articulate your emotions?

134. Create a relaxing bedtime routine

Why: A good night's rest can set you up for an emotionally balanced day. A good bedtime ritual helps with that.

Time: 30-60 minutes.

Tools: Practices like reading, gentle stretches, or meditation.

How: Incorporate calming activities before bed. Whatever activity you choose, do it consistently.

How did creating a relaxing bedtime routine improve your sleep patterns and support your emotional well-being?

135. Create a playlist of calming music

Why: Having a playlist of calming music on hand will make it easy for you to use this tool when you need it.

Time: 30-60 minutes.

Tools: Music streaming service, device for playback.

How: Choose a music streaming service and create a new playlist. Search for music that has a slow tempo, soft melodies, and harmonious sounds. Consider including genres like classical, jazz, ambient, or acoustic. Or, explore curated playlists on the platform for inspiration. Visit www.SandyRossAuthor.com/resources for suggestions.

How did creating and listening to a playlist of calming music affect your ability to relax and your overall mood?

136. Create a list of personal development books to read

Why: Creating a reading list can help you stay organized and focused on your self-improvement goals. It provides a clear plan for ongoing personal growth and learning.

Time: 30-60 minutes.

Tools: Internet access, paper and pen or digital device.

How: Research and compile a list of personal development books that interest you. Look for recommendations online, ask friends, or check bestseller lists. Write down the titles and authors, and prioritize them based on your interests and goals.

How did creating a list of personal development books to read impact your motivation and planning for personal growth?

137. Join an emotional check-in group

Why: Sharing your feelings with a group can provide support and reduce feelings of isolation. It helps you connect with others and gain different perspectives on emotional experiences.

Time: 30-60 minutes.

Tools: Online meeting platform or in-person group. Visit www.SandyRossAuthor.com/resources for suggestions.

How: Find or form a group that meets regularly for emotional check-ins. Share your feelings and listen to others, offering support and empathy.

How did participating in an emotional check-in group affect your sense of connection and emotional well-being?

138. Bake something simple

Why: Baking can be a therapeutic and rewarding activity that promotes relaxation and creativity. It also provides a delicious treat to enjoy.

Time: 30-60 minutes.

Tools: Ingredients for a simple recipe, oven.

How: Choose a simple baking recipe, such as cookies or muffins. Gather your ingredients, follow the recipe, and enjoy the process of baking.

How did baking something simple affect your mood and sense of accomplishment?

CHAPTER 8

SELF-CARE FOR YOUR SOUL

Your soul is your immaterial essence. It is the unique expression of you as a divine being, your life force. Taking care of your soul is doing what you need to do to make sure this life force thrives. Most of the activities you will find in this chapter have to do with reaching outside of yourself as a way to recharge yourself. Think of it this way - everyone you meet has a soul. Helping them puts your spiritual principles into practice and grows your connection to the divine.

To get you started, here are some affirmations for your soul:

- I am in tune with the transcendent and all that is around me.
- I am an infinite and abundant expression of love by design.
- I attract and radiate peace and joy.
- I choose to forgive and let go so that my soul can be free from unforgiveness.
- My soul is free. I am at peace with the divine plan for my life.

The Activities

139. Say no to something you don't want in your life

Why: Setting boundaries preserves your time and energy for priorities.

Time: Less than 5 minutes.

Tools: Assertiveness.

How: Recognize when something doesn't align with your values or goals. Politely decline without guilt or over-explanation.

How did saying no empower you to focus on what matters most? How did it impact your sense of control and well-being?

140. Intentionally wish happiness for others

Why: Wishing happiness for others can increase your own feelings of compassion and joy. It helps you cultivate a positive and empathetic mindset.

Time: Less than 5 minutes.

Tools: Mindfulness, compassion.

How: As you go about your day, intentionally observe people around you, whether you know them or not. Silently wish them happiness and well-being.

How did wishing happiness for others impact your own mood and outlook?

141. Practice gratitude at meals

Why: Expressing gratitude at meals can make you more mindful of your blessings. It fosters a habit of appreciation and positivity.

Time: Less than 5 minutes.

Tools: None.

How: Before eating, take a moment to express gratitude for your food and the people who made it possible.

How did practicing gratitude at meals affect your appreciation of your food and those around you?

142. Capture moments of spiritual insight

Why: Recording spiritual insights can deepen your understanding and connection to your spiritual journey. It helps you reflect on and integrate these insights into your daily life.

Time: 5-10 minutes.

Tools: Journal or notes app.

How: Whenever you experience a moment of spiritual clarity or insight, jot down your thoughts or feelings in a journal or notes app.

How did capturing your spiritual insights help you feel more connected to your spiritual journey?

143. Imagine you're your best friend

Why: If you were your best friend, what would you tell yourself right now? Look in the mirror and say it. Practicing self-compassion and positive self-talk boosts self-esteem and emotional well-being.

Time: 5-10 minutes.

Tools: Mirror.

How: Stand in front of a mirror. Imagine you're your best friend offering supportive words or a pep talk. Speak kindly to yourself.

How did practicing self-compassion in this way impact your self-perception or mood?

144. Lift someone up by sharing their work on social media

Why: Sharing someone's work promotes their talent and boosts their morale. The act of sharing without expecting anything in return nourishes your soul.

Time: 5-10 minutes.

Tools: Social media platforms (Facebook, Instagram, Twitter).

How: Share a friend or colleague's project, artwork, or achievement on your social media. Add a supportive and relevant comment.

How did sharing their work contribute to their recognition or success? How did it feel to support someone in this way?

145. Make a small connection

Why: Connecting with others fosters social bonds and brightens their day.

Time: 5-10 minutes.

Tools: Opportunity for interaction.

How: Strike up a friendly conversation with a sales assistant or barista. Show interest and appreciation for their service.

How did this brief interaction affect your and their mood? Did it create a positive exchange?

146. Reflect on your spiritual journey

Why: Reflecting on your spiritual journey can bring clarity and peace. It helps you reconnect with your core beliefs and values.

Time: 10-20 minutes.

Tools: Journal or quiet space.

How: Take some time to think about your spiritual beliefs and experiences. Write down any thoughts or feelings that arise.

How did reflecting on your spiritual journey make you feel?

147.   Spend time with animals

Why: Interacting with animals can reduce stress and boost mood. Animals' clear and positive emotions can bring a sense of calm and joy.

Time: 10-20 minutes.

Tools: None or visit an animal shelter, friend's pet, or local park.

How: Spend time playing with a pet if you have one, or visit a friend's pet, a local animal shelter, a pet café or a park where you can observe and interact with animals.

How did spending time with animals and their clear, positive emotions affect your mood and stress levels?

148.   Create a daily ritual for reflection

Why: A daily ritual for reflection can provide a consistent time for introspection and spiritual growth. It helps integrate mindfulness into your routine.

Time: 10-20 minutes.

Tools: Journal, quiet space.

How: Set aside time each day to reflect on your thoughts, feelings, and experiences. Use a journal to document your reflections and any insights gained.

How did creating a daily ritual for reflection impact your spiritual growth and mind?

149. Visualize a money tree

Why: Visualizing a money tree can help you conceptualize your financial growth and stability. This mental exercise promotes a positive financial mindset and can lead to more thoughtful financial planning. It encourages you to nurture your finances just as you would care for a growing plant.

Time: 10-20 minutes.

Tools: Quiet space, optional meditation music.

How: Find a quiet place where you can relax without interruptions. Close your eyes and imagine a tree where each leaf represents a financial asset or stream of income. Envision this tree growing in a healthy, fertile environment, with each branch expanding and each leaf flourishing. Think about the actions you take to water and nurture this tree, such as saving, investing, and making wise financial decisions.

How did visualizing your money tree influence your feelings about your financial situation and your future financial planning?

150. Maintain a hope journal

Why: A hope journal helps you focus on positive future possibilities. It encourages optimism and resilience.

Time: 10-20 minutes.

Tools: Journal, pen.

How: Regularly write down your hopes, dreams, and positive affirmations.

How did maintaining a hope journal affect your outlook on the future?

151. Practice self-compassion meditation

Why: Self-compassion meditation fosters kindness toward yourself and reduces self-criticism. It promotes emotional healing and resilience.

Time: 10-20 minutes.

Tools: Quiet space, meditation guide or recording.

How: Find a quiet space, sit comfortably, and follow a self-compassion meditation guide or recording. Focus on treating yourself with kindness and understanding.

How did practicing self-compassion meditation affect your relationship with yourself?

152. Explore different spiritual principles

Why: Learning about various spiritual principles can broaden your perspective and deepen your understanding of different beliefs. It can enhance your personal growth and spiritual journey.

Time: 20-30 minutes.

Tools: Internet, books, or articles on spiritual principles.

How: Research different spiritual principles from various cultures and traditions. Reflect on the ones that resonate with you and consider how they can be applied in your life.

How did learning about different spiritual principles influence your spiritual perspective?

153.   Write a letter to your future self

Why: Writing to your future self can provide clarity and set intentions for your spiritual journey. It encourages self-reflection and long-term thinking.

Time: 20-30 minutes.

Tools: Paper and pen.

How: Write a heartfelt letter to your future self, detailing your hopes and goals. Seal it and set a date to open it.

How did writing to your future self-help clarify your goals?

154.   Read a spiritually enriching text

Why: Reading spiritually enriching texts can provide insight, comfort, and inspiration. It helps deepen your understanding of life's profound questions and nurtures your soul.

Time: 20-30 minutes.

Tools: Book or online text.

How: Choose a text that resonates with you, such as poetry, philosophy, or spiritual writings. Find a quiet place and spend some time reading and reflecting on the message.

How did reading the text impact your thoughts and feelings about your spiritual journey?

155. Watch the sunrise or sunset

Why: Observing the sunrise or sunset can bring a sense of peace and wonder. It connects you to the natural rhythms of the world.

Time: 20-30 minutes.

Tools: Outdoor space with a clear view.

How: Find a comfortable spot to watch the sunrise or sunset, and take in the beauty.

How did watching the sunrise or sunset affect your mood and sense of connection to nature?

156. Perform a cleansing ritual

Why: A cleansing ritual can help you release negative energy and promote a sense of renewal. It can be a symbolic way to let go of what no longer serves you.

Time: 20-30 minutes.

Tools: Sage, incense, or essential oils.

How: Use sage, incense, or essential oils to cleanse your space. Move through each room with your chosen cleansing tool, setting the intention to release negativity.

How did performing a cleansing ritual affect your sense of clarity and renewal?

157. Create a gratitude jar

Why: A gratitude jar is a visual reminder of the positive aspects of your life. It helps cultivate a habit of gratitude and positivity.

Time: 20-30 minutes.

Tools: Jar, paper, pen.

How: Write down things you are grateful for on small pieces of paper and place them in a jar. Review them whenever you need a positivity boost.

How did creating and using a gratitude jar affect your outlook on life?

158. Make a list of tourist attractions in your town/state

Why: Creating a list of local attractions can help you appreciate the beauty and uniqueness of your surroundings. It encourages mindfulness and gratitude for the place you live in.

Time: 20-30 minutes.

Tools: Paper, pen, internet access.

How: Research online or think about popular tourist spots in your town or state. Write down a list of these attractions, including parks, museums, landmarks, and events.

How did making a list of local attractions affect your sense of gratitude and connection to your town/state?

159. Explore spiritual symbols and their meanings

Why: Learning about spiritual symbols can deepen your understanding of different cultures and beliefs. It can also enhance your own spiritual journey by finding symbols that resonate with you.

Time: 30-60 minutes.

Tools: Internet, books, or articles on spiritual symbols.

How: Research symbols across different cultures and spiritual traditions. Reflect on their significance in your spiritual journey.

How do spiritual symbols enrich your spiritual practice and understanding of the world?

160. Plan a two-day holiday for one weekend

Why: Taking a short break promotes relaxation and exploration without leaving town. Planning for it signals to yourself that you matter enough to care for.

Time: 30-60 minutes.

Tools: Calendar, maps, local guides.

How: Choose dates for a mini-holiday. Plan activities like visiting local attractions, trying new restaurants, or exploring parks.

What did planning your holiday teach you about yourself? Did you enjoy planning? Did you struggle identifying things you might enjoy?

161. Take a walk or ride with no destination

Why: Taking an aimless walk or ride can clear your mind and provide a sense of freedom and adventure. It allows you to disconnect from daily stresses and enjoy the present moment.

Time: 30-60 minutes.

Tools: Comfortable shoes, bike or car, or public transportation pass.

How: Go for a walk, bike ride, drive, or use public transportation with no specific destination in mind. Explore new areas and enjoy the journey.

How did taking an aimless walk or ride help you feel more relaxed and free?

162. Curate a spiritual playlist

Why: Music can be a powerful tool for relaxation and reflection. Creating a playlist of spiritually uplifting songs can help center your mind and elevate your mood.

Time: 30-60 minutes.

Tools: Music streaming service or library.

How: Select songs that inspire and uplift you, and create a playlist. Listen to it during quiet times.

How did listening to your spiritual playlist affect your mood and focus?

163. Craft a mini altar

Why: Creating a personal altar can provide a dedicated space for reflection and meditation. It helps to focus your spiritual practice and brings a sense of peace.

Time: 30-60 minutes.

Tools: Small table or shelf, meaningful items.

How: Arrange items that hold spiritual significance to you on a small table or shelf. Use this space for meditation or reflection.

How did having a mini altar influence your spiritual practice?

164. Photograph something beautiful

Why: Capturing beauty through photography can enhance your appreciation for the world around you. It promotes mindfulness and creativity.

Time: 30-60 minutes.

Tools: Camera or smartphone.

How: Spend time taking photos of things you find beautiful. Reflect on why they inspire you.

How did photographing something beautiful affect your appreciation of your surroundings?

165. Create a 'peace corner'

Why: A dedicated space for relaxation can provide a retreat from daily stress. It promotes mindfulness and a sense of calm.

Time: 30-60 minutes.

Tools: Comfortable seating, soft lighting, meaningful objects.

How: Set up a corner in your home with comfortable seating and items that promote peace. Use it for relaxation or meditation.

How did having a peace corner impact your stress levels?

166. Assemble a serenity kit

Why: A serenity kit can provide immediate comfort during stressful times. It includes items that calm and soothe you.

Time: 30-60 minutes.

Tools: Small bag or box, comforting items.

How: Gather items like essential oils, calming tea, and soft fabrics into a kit for easy access during stressful moments.

How did having a serenity kit affect your ability to manage stress?

167.　Craft your personal mantra

Why: Creating a personal mantra can provide guidance and focus. It serves as a reminder of your values and goals.

Time: 30-60 minutes.

Tools: Paper, pen.

How: Reflect on your core values and goals, then create a short, meaningful mantra. Repeat it daily.

How did crafting and using your personal mantra influence your daily mindset?

168.　Take yourself on a self-date

Why: Spending quality time with yourself can boost self-love and happiness. It allows you to enjoy your own company and do activities that you love.

Time: 1-2 hours.

Tools: Any activity you enjoy.

How: Plan a special activity just for yourself, like going to a café, visiting a museum, taking a walk in the park, or watching a movie. Treat yourself as you would on a date.

How did spending quality time with yourself make you feel?

169. Bake cookies and share with a loved one

Why: Acts of kindness can boost your mood and foster a sense of connection. Sharing homemade treats spreads joy and strengthens relationships.

Time: 1-2 hours.

Tools: Baking ingredients, oven, packaging.

How: Bake a batch of cookies and package them nicely. Leave them at a loved one's door with a kind note.

How did performing this act of kindness affect your mood and sense of connection?

170. Schedule quality time with positive people

Why: Spending time with positive and supportive people can boost your mood and reduce stress. It helps reinforce healthy relationships and personal happiness.

Time: 1-2 hours.

Tools: Phone or messaging app.

How: Plan a meet-up, call, or video chat with a friend or family member who makes you feel good. Prioritize this interaction over less positive ones.

How did spending time with someone positive affect your mood and overall well-being?

171. Join in a community or cultural event

Why: Attending community or cultural events can develop a sense of belonging and enrich your spiritual well-being. It provides an opportunity to connect with others and experience diverse traditions.

Time: 1-2 hours.

Tools: Local event listings.

How: Find and attend a community or cultural event such as a festival, solstice celebration, or public meditation session.

How did participating in the event affect your sense of connection, well-being or spiritual growth?

172. Craft a dream catcher

Why: Making a dream catcher can be a creative and meditative process. It is also a meaningful way to protect your sleeping space.

Time: 1-2 hours.

Tools: Hoop, string, beads, feathers.

How: Follow a tutorial to create a dream catcher with materials of your choice.

How did crafting a dream catcher make you feel, and how did it affect your sleep?

173. Organize a community sharing circle

Why: Sharing circles can build community and provide mutual support. They encourage open communication and shared experiences.

Time: 1-2 hours.

Tools: Meeting space, participants.

How: Invite people to join a sharing circle where everyone takes turns speaking and listening. Visit www.SandyRossAuthor.com/resources for suggestions.

How did participating in a sharing circle impact your sense of community?

174. Decorate with meaningful symbols

Why: Surrounding yourself with meaningful symbols can remind you of your values and goals. It enhances your living space with positive energy.

Time: 1-2 hours.

Tools: Decorative items, symbols, art supplies.

How: Choose symbols that resonate with you and incorporate them into your decor.

How did decorating with meaningful symbols influence your living environment and mood?

175. Create a zen garden

Why: Making a Zen garden can be a meditative and calming activity. It provides a serene space for reflection and relaxation.

Time: 1-2 hours.

Tools: Sand, small rocks, container, rake.

How: Design and create a small Zen garden in a container. Arrange the sand and rocks mindfully.

How did creating and maintaining a Zen garden influence your sense of calm?

176. Plant a tree

Why: Planting a tree can symbolize growth and renewal. It contributes positively to the environment and provides a sense of accomplishment.

Time: 1-2 hours.

Tools: Tree sapling, shovel, water.

How: Choose a suitable location and plant a tree. Care for it as it grows.

How did planting a tree and watching it grow affect your sense of purpose and connection to nature?

177. Visit a popular tourist attraction from your list

Why: Visiting a local attraction can provide a new perspective and create a sense of wonder and appreciation for your environment. It's a soulful way to connect with your surroundings and find beauty in the familiar.

Time: 1-2 hours.

Tools: Comfortable shoes, camera or smartphone.

How: Choose one attraction from your list and plan a visit. Spend time exploring mindfully, taking in the sights, sounds, and atmosphere with a sense of curiosity and wonder.

How did visiting a popular tourist attraction with a mindful approach affect your sense of wonder and appreciation for your town?

178. Build a 'feel good' file

Why: A feel good file can provide a boost of positivity when you need it. It serves as a reminder of your achievements and happy moments.

Time: 1-2 hours.

Tools: Folder or box, positive mementos.

How: Collect positive notes, achievements, and mementos, and store them in a dedicated file.

How did revisiting your feel good file affect your mood and confidence?

179. Create a reflective scrapbook or photo album of your visit

Why: Creating a reflective scrapbook or photo album helps preserve meaningful memories and provides a space for contemplation and gratitude. It allows you to reflect on your experiences and deepen your connection to your surroundings.

Time: 1-2 hours.

Tools: Photos, scrapbook or photo album, decorative materials.

How: Print out photos from your visit and gather any memorabilia like tickets or brochures. Arrange them in a scrapbook or photo album, adding thoughtful captions, dates, and personal reflections on the experience.

How did creating a reflective scrapbook or photo album enhance your sense of connection and gratitude for your experiences?

180. Participate in a charity event

Why: Participating in charity events can foster a sense of community and purpose. It allows you to contribute positively to the world around you.

Time: 2+ hours.

Tools: Local charity event listings.

How: Find a local charity event and sign up to participate.

How did participating in the charity event affect your sense of purpose and community?

181. Attend a workshop or retreat

Why: Attending workshops or retreats can provide new perspectives and deepen your spiritual practice. It offers a break from routine and a chance to connect with others.

Time: 2+ hours.

Tools: Workshop or retreat information.

How: Find a workshop or retreat that interests you and attend it. Engage fully in the experience.

How did attending the workshop or retreat impact your spiritual growth?

182. Host a meaningful conversation dinner

Why: Hosting a dinner with meaningful conversations can strengthen relationships and provide deeper connections. It fosters open dialogue and understanding.

Time: 2+ hours.

Tools: Meal, comfortable space, conversation topics.

How: Invite friends or family for dinner and discuss meaningful topics. Encourage everyone to share.

How did hosting a meaningful conversation dinner affect your relationships and understanding of others?

183. Personal retreat day

Why: Taking a day for yourself can rejuvenate your mind, body, and spirit. It provides an opportunity for deep reflection and self-care.

Time: One day.

Tools: Comfortable space, activities of choice.

How: Plan a day where you focus solely on activities that nurture your soul.

How did spending a personal retreat day impact your well-being?

CHAPTER 9

SELF-CARE IN YOUR RELATIONSHIPS

Good relationships are important for your well-being and need regular attention. This chapter is about nurturing your relationships and building supportive networks. You'll explore activities to support and grow respectful intimate partnerships, friendships, family relationships, and work relationships.

To kick you off, here are some related affirmations:

- I deserve fulfilling relationships.
- I am grateful for the people who love me.
- My love is precious. I spread love. It returns to me.
- I share a deep, and loving connection with my friends.
- I have the right to choose connections that are healthy for me.

The Activities

184. Compliment someone

Why: Giving a genuine compliment can boost the recipient's mood and self-esteem. It also strengthens your connection with them.

Time: Less than 5 minutes.

Tools: None.

How: Think of something positive and specific about the person. Deliver the compliment sincerely in person or via message.

How did complimenting someone affect your mood and your connection with them?

185. Send a funny meme or video to a friend

Why: Sharing humor can lighten the mood and strengthen bonds. It shows you're thinking of them and want to share joy.

Time: Less than 5 minutes.

Tools: Your choice of device, internet access.

How: Find a funny meme or video that you think your friend will enjoy and send it to them.

How did sharing a funny meme or video affect your relationship and mood?

186. Express appreciation to a colleague

Why: Expressing appreciation at work can improve morale and teamwork. It fosters a positive and supportive work environment.

Time: 5-10 minutes.

Tools: None.

How: Write a quick note or verbally express your appreciation for a colleague's help or effort.

How did expressing appreciation to a colleague affect your work relationship and atmosphere?

187. Send an encouraging message

Why: Sending encouragement can uplift someone and show your support. It strengthens positive connections and boosts morale.

Time: 5-10 minutes.

Tools: Phone or messaging app.

How: Send a message of encouragement to a friend or family member who may need it.

How did sending an encouraging message affect your relationship and the recipient's mood?

188. Send a thank-you note

Why: Expressing gratitude strengthens relationships and makes others feel appreciated. It can brighten someone's day and foster positive feelings.

Time: 10-20 minutes.

Tools: Thank-you card, pen.

How: Write a heartfelt thank-you note to someone who has helped you or been kind to you. Mail or hand-deliver the note.

How did sending a thank-you note affect your feelings and your relationship with the recipient?

189. Share a positive memory with someone

Why: Sharing positive memories can strengthen bonds and bring joy. It reinforces your connection and shared history.

Time: 10-20 minutes.

Tools: None.

How: Think of a happy memory you shared with someone and recount the story to them.

How did sharing a positive memory affect your relationship and emotions?

190. Reconnect with an old friend via message

Why: Reconnecting with old friends can revive meaningful relationships. It can bring joy and a sense of continuity.

Time: 10-20 minutes.

Tools: Messaging app or social media.

How: Send a message to an old friend, mentioning a shared memory or asking how they've been.

How did reconnecting with an old friend affect your sense of connection and nostalgia?

191. Share a favorite book or article

Why: Sharing something you enjoy can provide common ground and spark interesting discussions. It shows that you value the other person's interests.

Time: 10-20 minutes.

Tools: Book or article link.

How: Recommend a favorite book or article to a friend, explaining why you think they'd like it.

How did sharing a favorite book or article affect your conversations and connection with the recipient?

192. Celebrate someone's achievement

Why: Celebrating others' achievements shows you care and are genuinely happy for them. It strengthens positive feelings and mutual respect.

Time: 10-20 minutes.

Tools: Card or message.

How: Congratulate someone on their achievement with a card, message, or small celebration.

How did celebrating someone's achievement affect your relationship and their feelings?

193. Ask About someone's day

Why: Asking about someone's day shows you care and are interested in their life. It strengthens bonds and promotes open communication.

Time: 10-20 minutes.

Tools: None.

How: During a conversation, ask how their day was and listen attentively to their response.

How did asking about someone's day affect your understanding and connection with them?

194. Give someone a book recommendation

Why: Sharing a book recommendation can spark interesting discussions and show you care about their interests. It provides a personal touch to your connection.

Time: 10-20 minutes.

Tools: Book title or link.

How: Recommend a book you think the other person will enjoy and explain why.

How did giving a book recommendation affect your conversations and connection with the recipient?

195. Share a podcast or music recommendation

Why: Sharing media recommendations can create common ground and spark discussions. It shows you care about their interests.

Time: 10-20 minutes.

Tools: Podcast or music streaming service.

How: Recommend a podcast or music album you think the other person will enjoy and explain why.

How did sharing a podcast or music recommendation affect your conversations and connection with the recipient?

196. Make a list of important dates for your relationships

Why: Remembering and acknowledging important dates shows you care and are attentive. It strengthens your bond and makes others feel valued.

Time: 10-20 minutes.

Tools: Calendar.

How: Note down important dates like birthdays or anniversaries in your calendar and acknowledge them when they come.

How did remembering and acknowledging important dates affect your relationships and their feelings of appreciation?

197. Leave a positive review for a friend's business

Why: Supporting a friend's business shows you care about their success. It can boost their confidence and strengthen your bond.

Time: 10-20 minutes.

Tools: Internet access.

How: Write and post a positive review for a friend's business online.

How did leaving a positive review for a friend's business affect your relationship and their business?

198. Share a recipe

Why: Sharing a recipe can provide a fun way to bond and exchange culinary skills. It shows thoughtfulness and can lead to enjoyable cooking experiences.

Time: 10-20 minutes.

Tools: Recipe card or email.

How: Write down or email a favorite recipe to a friend or family member.

How did sharing a recipe affect your relationship and the recipient's cooking experience?

199. Send a "Just Thinking of You" card

Why: Sending a card shows that you care and are thinking about someone. It can brighten their day and strengthen your bond.

Time: 10-20 minutes.

Tools: Card, pen, postage.

How: Write a heartfelt message in a "just thinking of you" card and mail it to a friend or family member.

How did sending a "just thinking of you" card affect your relationship and the recipient's mood?

200. Make a list of what you want in a relationship

Why: Clarifying what you want in a relationship can help you understand your needs and desires. It provides a foundation for building healthier and more fulfilling connections.

Time: 20-30 minutes.

Tools: Paper, pen.

How: Find a quiet place and take some time to reflect on what you value and need in a relationship. Write down the qualities and attributes that are important to you.

How did making a list of what you want in a relationship affect your understanding of your needs and desires?

201. Listen actively during a conversation

Why: Active listening shows respect and empathy. It enhances communication and understanding in relationships.

Time: 20-30 minutes.

Tools: None.

How: Focus on the speaker, make eye contact, and avoid interrupting. Reflect back what you heard to ensure understanding.

How did practicing active listening affect your conversations and relationships?

202. Make a joke book

Why: Creating a joke book can provide laughter and joy, which strengthens bonds and improves mood. It's a fun way to share humor and connect with others.

Time: 30-60 minutes.

Tools: Paper, pen, internet for joke research.

How: Collect your favorite jokes from books, the internet, or your own creations. Write them down in a notebook or create a digital document. Decorate the pages if you like.

How did making a joke book affect your mood and your relationships through shared laughter?

203. Make a list of what makes you a desirable partner

Why: Creating a list of your positive qualities will make you more self-aware and strengthen your confidence in a relationship.

Time: 30-60 minutes.

Tools: Pen and paper, journal.

How: Take a quiet moment to reflect on your strengths, values, and interests. Write down specific qualities and aspects that you believe make you a desirable partner. Review your list periodically to affirm these qualities and consider how they contribute to your relationships.

How did making a list of your desirable qualities boost your self-esteem?

204. Clarify your values

Why: Understanding and aligning with your values strengthens relationship compatibility and personal integrity.

Time: 30-60 minutes.

Tools: Journal, Reflection, introspection.

How: Reflect on what matters most to you in life and relationships. Write down your core values and consider how they guide your interactions.

How did clarifying your values leave you feeling? Do you generally act in alignment with your values or out of alignment?

205. Discover your love language

Why: Understanding and practicing each other's love languages can enhance emotional intimacy and communication.

Time: 30-60 minutes.

Tools: Love language quiz.

How: Take a love language quiz together to discover your primary love languages. The goal is to make a conscious effort to express love and appreciation in ways that resonate with each other.

What is your partner's primary love language? How can you practice it to better how you love them?

206. Call or FaceTime with family or friends

Why: Calling or FaceTiming family or friends nurtures relationships even when you are not close to each other and keeps connections strong.

Time: 30-60 minutes.

Tools: Phone or computer with internet access.

How: Schedule a call or FaceTime session with loved ones. Share updates, stories, and laughter. Take time to catch up and show you care about their lives.

How did calling or FaceTiming with family or friends strengthen your connections and sense of community?

207. Make a small gift for someone

Why: Giving a handmade gift shows thoughtfulness and care. It can strengthen your bond and make the recipient feel valued.

Time: 30-60 minutes.

Tools: Craft or baking supplies.

How: Create a small, thoughtful gift like a handmade card, a baked treat, or a simple craft.

How did making and giving a small gift affect your feelings and your relationship with the recipient?

208. Invite someone for a walk

Why: Inviting someone for a walk combines physical activity with social interaction. It can strengthen your bond and provide a relaxing environment for conversation.

Time: 30-60 minutes.

Tools: Comfortable shoes.

How: Invite a friend or family member for a walk in a park or around your neighborhood.

How did inviting someone for a walk affect your relationship and overall mood?

209. Help someone with a task

Why: Helping with a task can show your support and strengthen your bond. It demonstrates kindness and can make the other person's day easier.

Time: 30-60 minutes.

Tools: Depends on the task.

How: Offer to help someone with a task they need to complete, such as moving furniture, gardening, or running errands.

How did helping someone with a task affect your relationship and sense of purpose?

210. Share a homemade treat

Why: Sharing food is a traditional way to show care and strengthen bonds. It can bring joy and a sense of togetherness.

Time: 30-60 minutes.

Tools: Ingredients for a treat.

How: Make a simple homemade treat like cookies or bread and share it with someone.

How did sharing a homemade treat affect your relationship and feelings of connection?

211. Celebrate a small milestone together

Why: Celebrating small milestones can bring joy and strengthen your bond. It shows you appreciate and support each other's journey.

Time: 30-60 minutes.

Tools: Small gift or celebratory item.

How: Recognize and celebrate a small milestone in someone's life, like completing a project or achieving a personal goal.

How did celebrating a small milestone together affect your relationship and sense of support?

212. Offer to run an errand for someone

Why: Running an errand for someone shows kindness and support. It can relieve their stress and strengthen your bond.

Time: 30-60 minutes.

Tools: Depends on the errand.

How: Offer to run an errand for someone who may be busy or stressed, such as grocery shopping or picking up a package.

How did offering to run an errand for someone affect your relationship and their stress levels?

213. Create a playlist for a friend

Why: Sharing music can strengthen bonds and show you understand their tastes. It provides a personal touch and a thoughtful gift.

Time: 30-60 minutes.

Tools: Music streaming service.

How: Create a playlist with songs you think your friend will enjoy and share it with them.

How did creating and sharing a playlist affect your relationship and their enjoyment of music?

214. Support a friend's creative project

Why: Supporting a friend's project shows you care about their passions and efforts. It can boost their confidence and strengthen your bond.

Time: 30-60 minutes.

Tools: Depends on the project.

How: Offer help or encouragement for a friend's creative project, like providing feedback, sharing their work, or helping with tasks.

How did supporting a friend's creative project affect your relationship and their motivation?

215. Plan a future get-together

Why: Planning future activities gives you something to look forward to and strengthens your bond. It shows you value spending time together.

Time: 30-60 minutes.

Tools: Calendar.

How: Discuss and plan a future get-together, like a coffee date, hike, or meal.

How did planning a future get-together affect your relationship and anticipation for spending time together?

216. Send flowers or a small gift

Why: Sending a small gift can show your appreciation and make someone's day. It strengthens your bond and demonstrates thoughtfulness.

Time: 30-60 minutes.

Tools: Flowers or small gift.

How: Choose and send flowers or a small gift to someone as a surprise.

How did sending flowers or a small gift affect your relationship and the recipient's mood?

217. Create a shared playlist

Why: Making a shared playlist can strengthen bonds through mutual music interests. It provides a fun way to discover new music together.

Time: 30-60 minutes.

Tools: Music streaming service.

How: Use a music streaming service to create a collaborative playlist. Add songs you both enjoy and share them with each other.

How did creating a shared playlist affect your relationship and enjoyment of music?

218. Start a book exchange

Why: A book exchange can foster intellectual discussions and strengthen your bond. It provides a fun way to share and discover new books.

Time: 30-60 minutes.

Tools: Books.

How: Choose books you think the other person will enjoy and exchange them. Discuss your thoughts after reading.

How did starting a book exchange affect your relationship and conversations about books?

219. Write a joint bucket list

Why: Writing a joint bucket list can inspire shared goals and dreams. It strengthens your bond through mutual aspirations.

Time: 30-60 minutes.

Tools: Paper, pen.

How: Sit down together and brainstorm activities or goals you both want to achieve. Write them down in a joint bucket list.

How did writing a joint bucket list affect your relationship and shared sense of adventure?

220. Help a friend organize their space

Why: Helping a friend organize their space can show your support and strengthen your bond. It can make their life easier and more enjoyable.

Time: 1-2 hours.

Tools: Organizing supplies.

How: Offer to help a friend organize a part of their home, like a closet or pantry. Work together to declutter and arrange the space.

How did helping a friend organize their space affect your relationship and their sense of organization?

221. Send a surprise care package

Why: Sending a care package can show you care and provide a pleasant surprise. It strengthens your bond and shows thoughtfulness.

Time: 1-2 hours.

Tools: Care package items, box.

How: Gather items that the recipient will enjoy and pack them into a box. Send the care package with a personal note.

How did sending a surprise care package affect your relationship and the recipient's feelings?

222. Join a local community group together

Why: Joining a community group together can strengthen bonds and create a sense of belonging. It provides opportunities for shared activities and support.

Time: 1-2 hours.

Tools: Community group information.

How: Find a local community group that interests both of you and attend a meeting or event together.

How did joining a local community group together affect your sense of belonging and your relationship?

223. Invite someone to a game night, virtual or in person

Why: Game nights can provide fun and social interaction. They strengthen bonds and create shared experiences, even from a distance.

Time: 1-2 hours.

Tools: Board games or online game platform.

How: Plan and invite friends to a game night using an online platform or a board game. Choose games that everyone will enjoy.

How did inviting someone to a game night affect your relationship and shared enjoyment?

224. Host a movie night with friends

Why: Hosting a movie night can provide entertainment and strengthen social bonds. It creates a relaxed environment for connection.

Time: 1-2 hours.

Tools: Movie, snacks, comfortable seating.

How: Choose a movie and invite friends to watch it together, either in person or virtually. Prepare snacks and create a comfortable viewing area.

How did hosting a movie night with friends affect your relationships and enjoyment?

225. Organize a picnic

Why: Organizing a picnic can provide a relaxing and enjoyable outdoor experience. It strengthens your bond through shared meals and nature.

Time: 1-2 hours.

Tools: Picnic supplies, food.

How: Choose a park or outdoor location. Pack food, a blanket, and any other picnic essentials, and enjoy a meal together outdoors.

How did organizing a picnic affect your relationship and enjoyment of the outdoors?

226.   Create a photo album together

Why: Creating a photo album can provide a nostalgic and bonding experience. It preserves memories and strengthens your connection.

Time: 1-2 hours.

Tools: Photos, album, glue or digital tool.

How: Gather photos and spend time arranging them in an album, either physical or digital. Add captions and decorations as desired.

How did creating a photo album together affect your relationship and sense of shared memories?

227.   Collaborate on a DIY project

Why: Collaborating on a DIY project can provide a fun and productive bonding experience. It encourages teamwork and creativity.

Time: 1-2 hours.

Tools: DIY project materials.

How: Choose a simple DIY project, gather materials, and work on it together. Enjoy the process and the final result.

How did collaborating on a DIY project affect your relationship and sense of accomplishment?

228.   Host a potluck dinner

Why: Hosting a potluck dinner fosters community and strengthens social bonds. It provides an opportunity for shared meals and conversations.

Time: 2+ hours.

Tools: Food, dining space.

How: Invite friends or family to bring a dish to share. Set up a dining space and enjoy the meal together.

How did hosting a potluck dinner affect your relationships and sense of community?

Chapter 10

Self-Care at Work

A lot of times when people talk about self-care, they reserve it for outside work hours. But the reality of the matter is that work is invariably intertwined with our life routines. Self-care needs to get there too. How do you grind through a hard day without wearing yourself out? A good place is always to start with some affirmations:

- I am excited for the possibilities that today holds.
- I will be productive and wise with my time so I can achieve my goals.
- My work enhances my life, but does not define who I am.
- I am creating a work life that inspires and motivates me.
- My ability to conquer any challenge is limitless. I have an infinite potential for success.

Many people spend a third of their lives working so shelving self-care for after work isn't sustainable. But how do you integrate self-care into your work? This chapter answers that.

The Activities

229. Perform a quick posture check

Why: Maintaining good posture can prevent physical strain and improve comfort. It supports better breathing and reduces discomfort.

Time: Less than 5 minutes.

Tools: None.

How: Take a moment to check and adjust your posture, ensuring your back is straight and shoulders are relaxed.

How did checking and adjusting your posture affect your physical comfort and focus?

230. Reduce small distractions

Why: Minimizing distractions can significantly improve focus and productivity. It helps you stay on task and complete your work more efficiently.

Time: 5-10 minutes.

Tools: Quiet space, focus tools.

How: Identify common distractions and take steps to minimize them, such as turning off notifications and finding a quiet workspace.

How did reducing small distractions affect your productivity and focus?

231. Set up a social media blocker

Why: Blocking social media during work hours can help maintain focus and productivity. It reduces the temptation to check updates and allows you to stay on task.

Time: 5-10 minutes.

Tools: Social media blocking software or app.

How: Install and configure a social media blocker on your devices during work hours.

How did using a social media blocker impact your work focus and productivity?

232. Fight eye strain

Why: Reducing eye strain can improve comfort and productivity. It prevents headaches and fatigue associated with long screen time.

Time: 5-10 minutes.

Tools: None.

How: Follow the 20-20-20 rule: every 20 minutes, look at something 20 feet away for at least 20 seconds.

How did practicing the 20-20-20 rule affect your eye comfort and overall well-being?

233. Take a few minutes to get ready each day

Why: Starting your day by getting ready can boost your mood and prepare you for work. It sets a positive tone for the day.

Time: 5-10 minutes.

Tools: Grooming supplies.

How: Take time to freshen up, dress comfortably, and prepare yourself mentally for the day.

How did taking a few minutes to get ready each day affect your mood and readiness for work?

234. Build pauses into the workday

Why: Regular breaks can improve focus and prevent burnout. They help you recharge and maintain high productivity levels throughout the day.

Time: 5-10 minutes.

Tools: Timer or reminder app.

How: Schedule short breaks throughout your workday to rest and recharge.

How did building regular pauses into your day affect your energy and focus?

235.   Set communication time boundaries

Why: Setting boundaries for communication can help you manage your time and reduce stress. It ensures you have dedicated periods for focused work.

Time: 5-10 minutes.

Tools: Calendar or planner.

How: Allocate specific times for checking and responding to emails and messages. Stick to these times.

How did setting communication boundaries impact your focus and stress levels?

236.   Take a stretch break

Why: Stretching can reduce muscle tension and improve flexibility. It provides a quick way to relax and rejuvenate during the workday.

Time: 5-10 minutes.

Tools: None.

How: Stand up and perform simple stretches for your arms, legs, and back.

How did taking a stretch break affect your physical comfort and energy levels?

237. Visualization of achievement

Why: Visualizing success can increase motivation and focus. It helps you stay committed to your goals and boosts confidence.

Time: 5-10 minutes.

Tools: Quiet space.

How: Close your eyes and visualize yourself achieving a specific goal. Imagine the steps and the outcome.

How did visualizing achievement impact your motivation and focus?

238. Do a quick relaxation exercise

Why: A quick relaxation exercise can reduce stress and improve focus. It helps you stay calm and centered during the workday.

Time: 5-10 minutes.

Tools: Quiet space.

How: Sit quietly and practice deep breathing or a short guided relaxation exercise.

How did the relaxation exercise affect your stress levels and focus?

239. Environmental scan

Why: An environmental scan can help you stay aware of your surroundings and improve safety. It encourages mindfulness and attention to detail.

Time: 5-10 minutes.

Tools: None.

How: Take a few minutes to observe your workspace and surroundings. Note anything that needs adjustment or attention.

How did performing an environmental scan impact your awareness and focus?

240. Positive email to yourself

Why: Sending a positive email to yourself can boost your mood and motivation. It serves as a reminder of your strengths and achievements.

Time: 5-10 minutes.

Tools: Email account.

How: Write a positive, encouraging email to yourself highlighting your accomplishments and strengths.

How did receiving a positive email from yourself affect your mood and motivation?

241. Learn a new fact

Why: Learning something new can stimulate your mind and provide a break from routine tasks. It encourages curiosity and continuous learning.

Time: 5-10 minutes.

Tools: Internet or book.

How: Take a few minutes to learn a new fact or piece of information that interests you.

How did learning a new fact impact your curiosity and engagement?

242. Take a quiet moment for yourself

Why: Taking a quiet moment can reduce stress and improve focus. It provides a mental break and helps you relax.

Time: 5-10 minutes.

Tools: Quiet space.

How: Find a quiet place and take a few minutes to sit quietly, breathe deeply, and relax.

How did taking a quiet moment for yourself affect your stress levels and focus?

243. Recognize a colleague

Why: Recognizing a colleague's efforts can boost morale and strengthen work relationships. It fosters a positive and supportive work environment.

Time: 5-10 minutes.

Tools: None.

How: Take time to acknowledge and appreciate a colleague's hard work or achievements.

How did recognizing a colleague affect your relationship and the work environment?

244. Practice hand stretches

Why: Hand stretches can prevent stiffness and improve flexibility. They are especially helpful for those who use computers frequently.

Time: 5-10 minutes.

Tools: None.

How: Perform simple hand stretches, such as extending and flexing your fingers or gently pulling each finger back.

How did practicing hand stretches affect your comfort and flexibility?

245. Engage in a quick gratitude exercise

Why: A short gratitude exercise can boost your mood and reduce stress. It helps you focus on the positive aspects of your day.

Time: 5-10 minutes.

Tools: None.

How: Take a few minutes to think about or write down three things you are grateful for. Reflect on why you appreciate them.

How did the gratitude exercise affect your mood and perspective?

246. Watch a short educational video

Why: Watching an educational video can stimulate your mind and provide new insights. It helps you learn something new and stay engaged.

Time: 5-10 minutes.

Tools: Internet access.

How: Find a short educational video on a topic that interests you and watch it during a break.

How did watching the educational video affect your knowledge and engagement?

247.   Set daily intentions

Why: Setting daily intentions can increase focus and motivation. It helps you start your day with a clear purpose.

Time: 5-10 minutes.

Tools: Journal or notepad.

How: Write down your intentions for the day, focusing on what you want to achieve and how you want to feel.

How did setting daily intentions affect your focus and motivation for the day?

248.   Read an inspirational quote

Why: Reading inspirational quotes can boost your mood and provide motivation. It helps you stay positive and focused on your goals.

Time: 5-10 minutes.

Tools: Inspirational book or online resource.

How: Read and reflect on a few inspirational quotes, considering how they apply to your life and goals.

How did reflecting on inspirational quotes affect your mood and motivation?

249.   Create a "one day" list

Why: Having a list of things you'd like to do someday can motivate you and give you something to look forward to. It helps you keep track of long-term goals and dreams.

Time: 10-20 minutes.

Tools: Paper and pen or digital note app.

How: Write down a list of activities or goals you want to achieve one day.

How did creating a "one day" list influence your motivation and outlook on future goals?

250.   Plan your workday the day before

Why: Planning ahead can help you start your day with clear goals and priorities. It reduces morning stress and increases productivity.

Time: 10-20 minutes.

Tools: Planner or digital calendar.

How: At the end of each workday, plan and outline your tasks for the next day.

How did planning your workday the day before affect your morning routine and productivity?

251. Force yourself to brain dump

Why: Brain dumping helps clear your mind and organize your thoughts. It can reduce stress and improve focus.

Time: 10-20 minutes.

Tools: Paper and pen or digital note app.

How: Write down everything that's on your mind, from tasks to worries, to clear mental clutter.

How did brain dumping impact your mental clarity and stress levels?

252. Pack a nutritious and delicious lunch

Why: Eating a healthy lunch provides essential nutrients and sustained energy. It improves concentration and overall health.

Time: 10-20 minutes.

Tools: Healthy ingredients, lunch container.

How: Prepare a balanced lunch with proteins, vegetables, and whole grains.

How did packing and eating a nutritious lunch affect your energy and focus?

253. Ask for feedback

Why: Seeking feedback can help you improve your performance and build better relationships with colleagues. It provides valuable insights for personal and professional growth.

Time: 10-20 minutes.

Tools: Feedback form or direct conversation.

How: Ask a colleague or supervisor for constructive feedback on your work.

How did receiving feedback help you improve and feel more connected at work?

254. Mindful walking

Why: Mindful walking combines physical activity with mindfulness, reducing stress and improving mental clarity. It provides a break and a chance to refresh your mind.

Time: 10-20 minutes.

Tools: Comfortable shoes.

How: Take a walk, focusing on your surroundings and your breathing, without distractions.

How did mindful walking affect your stress levels and mental clarity?

255. Create a self-appreciation list

Why: A self-appreciation list can boost your confidence and motivation. It helps you recognize your strengths and achievements.

Time: 10-20 minutes.

Tools: Paper and pen.

How: Write down things you appreciate about yourself and your accomplishments. They may or may not be about work. Think broadly.

How did creating a self-appreciation list impact your self-esteem and motivation?

256. Deep listening

Why: Deep listening improves communication and strengthens relationships. It helps you understand others better and fosters empathy.

Time: 10-20 minutes.

Tools: None.

How: Engage in a conversation where you focus entirely on listening, without interrupting.

How did practicing deep listening affect your understanding and connection with others?

257. Declutter your workspace

Why: Keeping your workspace organized can reduce stress and improve efficiency. It creates a clean and productive environment.

Time: 10-20 minutes.

Tools: None.

How: Take time to clear away clutter, organize your materials, and clean your workspace.

How did decluttering your workspace impact your focus and productivity?

258. Check your comfort level

Why: Ensuring your workspace is comfortable can prevent physical strain and improve productivity. It supports better posture and reduces discomfort.

Time: 10-20 minutes.

Tools: Ergonomic checklist.

How: Assess your workspace setup and make adjustments for better ergonomics and comfort.

How did improving your workspace comfort affect your physical well-being and productivity?

259. Family or friend call

Why: Connecting with loved ones can boost your mood and provide emotional support. It strengthens relationships and reduces feelings of isolation.

Time: 10-20 minutes.

Tools: Phone.

How: Take a break to call a family member or friend and catch up.

How did talking to a loved one affect your mood and sense of connection?

260. Organize your task list

Why: Keeping your task list organized can reduce stress and improve efficiency. It helps you stay on top of your responsibilities.

Time: 10-20 minutes.

Tools: Paper and pen or digital task manager.

How: Review and organize your task list, prioritizing tasks and setting deadlines.

How did organizing your task list affect your productivity and stress levels?

261. Task batching

Why: Batching similar tasks together can improve efficiency and reduce mental fatigue. It helps streamline your workflow and manage time better.

Time: 10-20 minutes.

Tools: Task list.

How: Group similar tasks and schedule specific times to complete them in batches.

How did task batching affect your productivity and time management?

262. Create a DIY scented workspace spray

Why: A pleasant scent can boost mood and reduce stress. Creating your own spray allows you to personalize your workspace with a fragrance that helps you feel relaxed and focused.

Time: 10-20 minutes.

Tools: Spray bottle, water, optional: citrus peels, herbs, or essential oils.

How: Fill a spray bottle with water. Add citrus peels (like lemon or orange), fresh herbs (like mint or rosemary), or a few drops of essential oil if available. Shake well and spray around your workspace.

How did the scented spray affect your mood and work environment?

263. Clean out your email

Why: Keeping your email organized can reduce stress and improve efficiency. It helps you stay on top of important tasks and communications.

Time: 20-30 minutes.

Tools: Email software.

How: Delete unnecessary emails, organize important ones into folders, and respond to pending messages.

How did cleaning out your email affect your sense of organization and stress levels?

264. Use the Pomodoro Method

Why: The Pomodoro Method enhances focus and productivity through timed work intervals. It helps manage time effectively and reduce burnout.

Time: 20-30 minutes.

Tools: Timer.

How: Work for 25 minutes, then take a 5-minute break. Repeat this cycle and take a longer break after four sessions.

How did using the Pomodoro Method impact your productivity and focus?

265. Create a personal skills register and update it monthly

Why: Tracking your skills helps you recognize growth and identify areas for improvement. It can boost confidence and career development.

Time: 20-30 minutes.

Tools: Notebook or digital document.

How: List your skills and update it monthly with new ones you've developed. Reflect on your growth.

How did creating and updating your skills register impact your confidence and career development?

266. Digital clean-up

Why: Organizing your digital space can reduce stress and improve efficiency. It helps you find files and emails quickly, making your workday smoother.

Time: 20-30 minutes.

Tools: Computer or mobile device.

How: Delete unnecessary files and emails, organize your folders, and clean up your desktop.

How did cleaning up your digital space affect your efficiency and stress levels?

267. Listen to a motivational podcast

Why: Listening to a motivational podcast can provide inspiration and new insights. It helps you stay informed and inspired.

Time: 20-30 minutes.

Tools: Podcast app or website.

How: Find a podcast that interests you and listen during a break or while working on a routine task.

How did listening to a motivational podcast affect your mood and knowledge?

268. Focus Sprint

Why: Dedicating a short, focused burst of time to a single task can make it easier to tackle tasks that seem daunting. A sprint can also boost productivity, help break through procrastination, encourage deep work, and give you a sense of achievement

Time: 20-30 minutes.

Tools: Timer (e.g., smartphone timer, kitchen timer).

How: Select a task that has been pending or needs concentrated effort. Set your timer for 20 minutes. Remove distractions and check that you have all necessary materials at hand. Work intensely on the task until the timer goes off.

How did focusing intensely for 20 minutes impact your productivity and feelings towards the task?

269. Brainstorming session

Why: Brainstorming can boost creativity and problem-solving skills. It helps generate new ideas and solutions for your tasks.

Time: 20-30 minutes.

Tools: Paper and pen or whiteboard.

How: Set aside time for a brainstorming session on a specific project or problem. Write down all ideas without judgment.

How did the brainstorming session affect your creativity and problem-solving skills?

270. Personal goal setting

Why: Setting personal goals can provide direction and motivation. It helps you focus on what you want to achieve and create a plan to get there.

Time: 20-30 minutes.

Tools: Paper and pen or digital tool.

How: Write down your personal goals and create a plan for achieving them. Review and update regularly.

How did setting personal goals affect your motivation and sense of direction?

271. Decorate your workspace

Why: Personalizing your workspace can make you feel more comfortable and motivated. It creates a pleasant environment that can boost productivity.

Time: 30-60 minutes.

Tools: Decorative items, photos, plants.

How: Add personal touches to your workspace, such as photos, plants, or motivational quotes.

How did decorating your workspace affect your comfort and motivation at work?

272. Do your most important task first

Why: Tackling your most important task first can increase productivity and reduce stress. It ensures critical tasks are completed when your energy and focus are highest.

Time: 30-60 minutes.

Tools: Task list.

How: Identify your most important task and work on it first thing in the morning.

How did completing your most important task first affect your productivity and stress levels?

273. Lunch outside

Why: Eating lunch outside can provide a change of scenery and fresh air. It helps you relax and recharge during the workday.

Time: 30-60 minutes.

Tools: Lunch, outdoor space.

How: Take your lunch break outside, find a pleasant spot, and enjoy your meal.

How did having lunch outside affect your relaxation and energy levels?

274. Enrol in a soft skills development class

Why: Improving soft skills can enhance communication, teamwork, and overall job performance. It supports personal and professional growth.

Time: 1-2 hours.

Tools: Online course platform or local class.

How: Find and enroll in a class focused on soft skills such as communication, leadership, or time management.

How did the soft skills class improve your work interactions and performance?

CHAPTER 11

SELF-CARE WITH MONEY

Although initially self-care with money may not seem as comforting as getting a massage or a trip to the spa, there is a lot of reassurance to be had when you have your financial ducks in a row.

To get you in the right mindset, here are some relevant affirmations:

- Abundance is coming. I deserve and accept it.
- Money comes my way in both expected and unexpected ways.
- I am getting out of my own way when it comes to money.
- Today, I commit to living my financial dreams.
- I can balance my desire for more with gratitude for what I have. I am in charge of my money.

The Activities

275. Donate to a cause you care about

Why: Supporting a cause through donations can give you perspective and help you be involved in your community. It doesn't have to hurt your financial health though. You can budget for it.

Time: Less than 5 minutes.

Tools: Donation platform.

How: Choose a cause, set up a one-time payment or recurring donation and make sure to always have it in your budget.

How does giving back to your community enhance your sense of purpose?

276. Check your credit score

Why: Monitoring your credit score supports financial awareness and planning, essential for self-care through informed financial decisions.

Time: Less than 5 minutes.

Tools: Credit monitoring app or website.

How: Use a reputable credit monitoring service to check your score regularly.

How does monitoring your credit score contribute to your financial confidence?

277. Make an extra debt payment

Why: Paying down debt faster reduces financial stress and moves you closer to financial freedom. It's about taking proactive steps to improve your financial health.

Time: Less than 5 minutes.

Tools: Device to log in to bank account.

How: Allocate extra funds toward paying off debt beyond the minimum payment. It could be any of the money you have saved from canceled subscriptions or turned down expenses in activity 6.

How much closer are you to being debt-free?

278. Set yourself up to save on autopilot

Why: Automating savings makes it easier to build financial security over time. It's like setting a foundation for your future self to thrive financially. You eliminate having to do it manually every time you receive money.

Time: Less than 5 minutes.

Tools: Bank details.

How: Set up automatic savings transfers or round-up features with your bank account.

How does saving on an autopilot make you feel?

279. Follow a money blog

Why: Following money blogs provides ongoing insights and tips for financial management, enhancing self-care through accessible information and guidance.

Time: 5-10 minutes.

Tools: Internet, RSS feed reader.

How: Subscribe to blogs that resonate with your financial goals, read updates regularly.

How does following money blogs improve your financial literacy and support your financial self-care practices?

280. Start tracking your expenses

Why: Tracking expenses increases financial awareness and accountability. It helps you manage your budget.

Time: 5-10 minutes.

Tools: Expense tracking app, notebook.

How: Use an app or notebook to record daily expenses, categorize spending, and analyze patterns after a month or so.

How does tracking expenses improve your financial habits?

281.   Install a shopping app to save money

Why: Using shopping apps saves money on purchases, stretching your budget and promoting financial mindfulness.

Time: 5-10 minutes.

Tools: Smartphone, app store.

How: Download a relevant shopping app, explore deals and cashback offers before shopping online or in-store.

How did your chosen shopping app affect your spending?

282.   Find a Groupon to save on an upcoming special event

Why: Finding Groupons for events saves money while enjoying experiences.

Time: 5-10 minutes.

Tools: Groupon app or website.

How: Browse Groupon for deals on activities or events you plan to attend.

How does using Groupon enhance your ability to enjoy special events while managing your budget?

283. Set a weekly savings goal

Why: Encourages consistent saving habits. Small, regular contributions can add up significantly over time, building a strong savings habit.

Time: 5-10 minutes.

Tools: Saving account, piggy bank or savings envelope.

How: Decide on an amount to save each week and set it aside.

Did setting a weekly goal make saving easier?

284. Write a money mantra

Why: Positive affirmations can improve your financial mindset. Repeating a money mantra can reduce financial anxiety and increase confidence.

Time: 5-10 minutes.

Tools: Paper and pen.

How: Create a short, positive statement about money and repeat it daily.

How does your money mantra influence your financial behavior?

285. Learn something new about money

Why: Increasing your financial knowledge builds confidence and empowers you to make informed decisions. It expands your understanding and helps you take control of your financial future.

Time: 10-20 minutes.

Tools: Money management book, online articles or blogs.

How: Explore topics like investments, savings strategies, or financial planning. Educate yourself through books, articles, or online courses.

What did you learn that you can start implementing with your money today?

286. Find and cancel recurring charges for things you aren't using

Why: Letting go of unused subscriptions frees up your money for things that matter more to you. It's like decluttering your finances for a clearer financial path.

Time: 10-20 minutes.

Tools: Bank statement.

How: Review your bank statements for recurring charges (like subscriptions or memberships) you no longer use or need. Take action to cancel them.

How much did you free up by canceling subscriptions you don't need?

287. Set up due date alerts

Why: Setting up due date alerts ensures timely bill payments, reducing late fees and promoting peace of mind in financial management.

Time: 10-20 minutes

Tools: Banking app or online account settings

How: Log into your bank or credit card account, enable alerts for bill due dates.

How do due date alerts enhance your awareness of financial responsibilities and support your peace of mind?

288. Make use of discounts and vouchers

Why: Utilizing discounts saves money on purchases, stretching your budget and promoting financial mindfulness.

Time: 10-20 minutes

Tools: Coupon apps, discount websites

How: Browse for discounts and vouchers before making purchases online or in-store.

How does using discounts contribute to your financial well-being?

289. Reflect on a past money mistake

Why: Acknowledging and forgiving past financial mistakes can relieve emotional burdens and pave the way for proactive money management.

Time: 10-20 minutes.

Tools: Journal or digital document.

How: Reflect on a specific financial error, understand what went wrong, learn from it, and consciously forgive yourself.

How does forgiving yourself influence your current financial attitudes?

290. Update financial account recipients

Why: Ensures that your financial assets are distributed according to your current wishes in the event of unforeseen circumstances.

Time: 10-20 minutes.

Tools: Account information, online banking or provider forms.

How: Review and update the beneficiary information on all your financial accounts, including insurance policies and retirement plans.

How does updating your beneficiaries reflect on your responsibilities?

291. Set some money intentions

Why: Setting intentions gives you clarity and direction. It's about focusing your efforts on what truly matters to you and aligning your actions with your aspirations.

Time: 10-20 minutes.

Tools: Self-awareness, vulnerability.

How: Write down specific financial and work goals. Place them where you'll see them regularly. Refer to the SMART goal setting framework in Chapter 2.

What are your most important financial and work goals?

292. Listen to a local money podcast or two

Why: The keyword here is local. You want to understand what the thought leaders think about money and the state of your local economy and how it affects you. It educates and inspires financial decision-making.

Time: 10-20 minutes.

Tools: Podcast app, headphones.

How: Choose podcasts that align with your financial goals and interests, listen during commutes or downtime.

How do money podcasts enhance your financial knowledge?

293. Review your bank statements for errors

Why: Catching errors early can save money and prevent future issues. Regularly reviewing statements helps maintain financial accuracy and ensures all transactions are legitimate.

Time: 10-20 minutes.

Tools: Bank statements.

How: Look through recent bank statements and highlight any unfamiliar transactions.

Did you find any errors or suspicious activity?

294. Create a wishlist for big purchases

Why: Helps prioritize spending and save for important items. It allows for thoughtful consideration of what is truly needed or desired, preventing impulse purchases.

Time: 10-20 minutes.

Tools: Paper and pen or notes app.

How: Write down items you want to purchase and estimate their costs.

Does having a wishlist help you feel more in control of your spending?

295.   Review your financial goals

Why: Keeps goals top of mind and adjusts them as needed. Regular reviews help ensure progress and relevance of financial targets.

Time: 10-20 minutes.

Tools: Financial goals list.

How: Look over your financial goals and assess your progress.

Are your goals still relevant and achievable?

296.   Compare prices for a future purchase

Why: Helps make informed buying decisions and save money. It prevents overspending and encourages smart shopping practices.

Time: 10-20 minutes.

Tools: Internet, shopping apps.

How: Look up prices for an item you plan to buy and compare costs.

Did price comparison change your purchase decision?

297. Organize your wallet

Why: It makes it easier to manage cash and cards. An organized wallet can reduce stress and improve financial efficiency.

Time: 10-20 minutes.

Tools: Wallet.

How: Remove unnecessary items and organize cash and cards.

Did organizing your wallet help you feel more in control of your finances?

298. Research fees you pay - bank accounts, credit cards, etc.

Why: Understanding fees associated with bank accounts and credit cards can help you save money and be more financially mindful.

Time: 20-30 minutes.

Tools: Bank statements, financial institution websites.

How: Review your bank and credit card statements, note any fees charged, and research ways to minimize or eliminate them.

How does researching and managing fees improve your financial efficiency?

299.   Compare salaries with people doing similar work

Why: Comparing salaries with peers helps you know that you are getting fair compensation and are competitive.

Time: 20-30 minutes.

Tools: Colleague, industry contacts or online resources.

How: Approach a trusted colleague for a salary discussion to gain insights into market rates. If this is not possible, research online to see what people offering the same services you are in the same industry are making.

How did understanding salary benchmarks influence your work decisions?

300.   Familiarize yourself with common financial scams

Why: Learning about financial scams protects your assets and promotes financial security.

Time: 20-30 minutes.

Tools: Internet, financial fraud prevention resources.

How: Research common financial scams online, stay updated on new tactics, and learn how to recognize and avoid them.

What financial scams have you fallen for or almost done?

301. Visualize your retirement

Why: Visualizing retirement goals can improve your commitment to saving and planning. It will focus your financial choices.

Time: 20-30 minutes.

Tools: Visualization exercises, retirement planning tools.

How: Set aside quiet time, imagine your ideal retirement lifestyle – where would you live? How? What do you need to save now to get there?

How does visualizing your retirement enhance your motivation to save and plan for the future?

302. Check up on your invoices or pay slip

Why: Taking the time to look at your invoices and/or pay slips helps you make sure everything is as per your contracts. You can also track your changes over time.

Time: 20-30 minutes.

Tools: Accounting software, client records, pay slip.

How: Review outstanding invoices, follow up with clients promptly to maintain cash flow. If you have a pay slip, look at the last couple of month's pay slips. Is everything as per your work contracts?

What did you notice in your invoices or pay slips that you do not understand?

303. Find unclaimed or lost money you're owed

Why: Reclaiming lost monies can boost your financial resources and promote financial security.

Time: 20-30 minutes.

Tools: Unclaimed property websites.

How: Search online databases for unclaimed funds using your name and state of residence.

How does reclaiming unclaimed money improve your financial situation?

304. Adopt online security practices to protect your identity

Why: Securing your online identity safeguards your financial information and promotes peace of mind.

Time: 20-30 minutes.

Tools: Password manager, cybersecurity tips.

How: Use a password manager, enable two-factor authentication, and stay informed about cybersecurity best practices.

How do online security practices enhance your confidence in managing finances online?

305. Plan a budget-friendly meal

Why: Reduces food expenses and improves meal planning skills. It promotes healthier eating habits and mindful grocery shopping.

Time: 20-30 minutes.

Tools: Recipe resources, grocery list.

How: Find a cost-effective recipe and plan a meal using budget ingredients.

Did planning a budget-friendly meal help reduce your food costs?

306. Research free financial education resources

Why: Increases knowledge without spending money. It provides valuable information that can improve financial decision-making.

Time: 20-30 minutes.

Tools: Internet.

How: Look for free courses, webinars, or articles on financial topics.

What new resources did you find that could help you?

307. Make a list of all your regular expenses

Why: Having a clear overview of expenses aids in budget management and prevents late payments, which can lead to fees or damaged credit.

Time: 30-60 minutes.

Tools: Spreadsheet software or notebook.

How: Create a detailed list of each regular expense including the service provider, the amount due, and the due date. Keep this list updated regularly.

How has organizing your expenses changed your approach to budgeting?

308. Research ways to maximize your income

Why: Find ways that you can maximize your income or diversify its sources to increase your financial resources.

Time: 30-60 minutes.

Tools: Internet, financial planning guides.

How: Find side hustle ideas, or ways to invest in skills development to increase earning potential.

What practical ways have you found that you can use to increase your income?

309. Confidently return and refund items

Why: Returning items ensures your money isn't wasted on things you don't need. It's about valuing your financial resources and making sure they're working for you.

Time: 30-60 minutes.

Tools: Storage basket.

How: Gather items you've been meaning to return. Make a plan to return them promptly. You can even put them in your car or somewhere convenient to make it more likely you return them the next time you are going out.

What did you learn about yourself and the purchase choices you make from this exercise?

310. Make a budget

Why: Creating a budget provides clarity and control over your finances, fostering financial stability and supporting mindful spending.

Time: 30-60 minutes.

Tools: Budgeting template, financial statements.

How: Allocate time to list income sources, categorize expenses, and set savings goals using a budgeting template or app.

How does having a budget enhance your financial awareness and support your financial goals?

311.   Have regular money dates

Why: Scheduling regular money dates improves financial organization, decision-making and proactive financial management.

Time: 30-60 minutes.

Tools: Financial records, relaxation aids.

How: Set aside time weekly to review expenses, track progress on financial goals, and plan for upcoming expenses.

How do regular money dates enhance your financial awareness and support your financial goals?

312.   Set up a financial vision board

Why: Visualizing goals can increase motivation to achieve them. It provides a creative and tangible way to stay focused on long-term financial aspirations.

Time: 30-60 minutes.

Tools: Old magazines, scissors, glue, board.

How: Cut out images and words representing your financial goals and arrange them on a board.

How does visualizing your financial goals make you feel?

313. Create a monthly financial check-in routine

Why: Regular check-ins can keep finances on track. It allows for timely adjustments to budgets and financial goals.

Time: 30-60 minutes.

Tools: Calendar, financial documents.

How: Schedule a time each month to review your finances and set goals.

How did the check-in help you stay on top of your finances?

314. Review and optimize insurance and utility services

Why: Regularly reviewing and optimizing your insurance policies and utility services can lead to significant cost savings, ensuring you are getting the best value for your money. It also helps you stay informed about your current coverage and utility usage, making adjustments as necessary to fit changes in your life or budget.

Time: 1-2 hours.

Tools: Current insurance policies, utility bills, internet access for comparison shopping.

How: Collect all relevant documents for your insurance policies and utility bills, reviewing each for current rates and coverage details. Use online tools to compare offers from other providers and consider renegotiating terms or switching to more cost-effective options if beneficial.

What impact do you anticipate these changes will have on your budget?

315. Research books about managing money

Why: Educating yourself about financial management can provide strategies and knowledge to improve your financial health. There's a huge range of books on many financial topics and you can borrow them from your local library if you don't want to spend money on them.

Time: 1-2 hours.

Tools: Internet, library, bookstores.

How: Look up highly-rated books on financial management, select one that aligns with your interests or needs, and commit to reading it.

What key takeaways did you gain from the book?

316. Watch a financial documentary

Why: Documentaries are educational and can provide new financial insights. Sharing other people's stories can inspire you to change your financial behavior and improve your financial literacy.

Time: 1-2 hours.

Tools: Streaming service or library.

How: Choose a financial documentary and watch it.

What new information did you learn from the documentary?

317. Plan a no-spend weekend

Why: Planning a no-spend weekend give you a break from spending and encourages you to be creative in coming up with ideas. It can reset spending habits and help discover free or low-cost activities. You could take a nature hike, cook new recipes with ingredients you have at home, do gardening, set up a movie marathon, or visit a free museum or exhibit.

Time: Weekend.

Tools: None.

How: Plan activities that don't require spending money.

How did you feel after a no-spend weekend?

318. Track your spending for a month

Why: Tracking spending helps you understand where your money goes, identify unnecessary expenditures, and adjust habits to align with financial goals.

Time: Ongoing.

Tools: Spending tracking app, spreadsheet, or notebook.

How: Decide on a tracking method and start recording every expense today. Continue for at least a month.

What insights have you gained from tracking your spending?

319. Build your emergency fund

Why: Saving for an emergency fund provides financial security and peace of mind during unexpected life circumstances.

Time: Ongoing.

Tools: Savings account.

How: Determine a monthly savings goal toward your emergency fund and automate transfers to the dedicated savings account.

How does having an emergency fund contribute to your sense of financial safety?

Chapter 12

Self-Care in Your Space

There are visible and invisible aspects of self-care. The food you eat, how long you exercise and the hours of sleep you get are things you can touch and measure. The invisible aspects are things like how much you feel loved and understood, how kind you are to yourself, and the state of your environment and your personal space. Your space is vital for your well-being, sense of confidence and connectedness with the world.

Some helpful affirmations:

- My space is a reflection of my inner world. I choose to fill it with beauty and positivity.
- I am allowed to take up space and occupy my environment with my presence.
- My home is more organized and peaceful every day.
- I am worthy of a peaceful and organized environment, and I take care to maintain it.
- I release what no longer serves me, and make space for what brings me joy in my life and my environment.

The Activities

320. One-minute declutter a shelf

Why: Quickly decluttering a shelf can make your space look tidier. It gives you a sense of accomplishment and makes it easier to find things.

Time: Less than 5 minutes.

Tools: None.

How: Choose a shelf, remove unnecessary items, and put items back in an orderly fashion. Discard any items that don't belong or are no longer needed.

How did the one-minute declutter affect your sense of order and mental clarity?

321. Unsubscribe from a mailing list

Why: Reducing the number of unwanted emails can declutter your inbox and reduce stress. It helps you focus on important messages and improves digital organization.

Time: 5-10 minutes.

Tools: Email account.

How: Open your email and identify mailing lists you no longer need. Use the "unsubscribe" link typically found at the bottom of these emails to remove yourself from the list. Repeat this for multiple lists if needed.

How did unsubscribing from unwanted mailing lists affect your digital clutter and stress levels?

322. Water your plants

Why: Watering your plants keeps them healthy and vibrant. It adds greenery to your space, which can improve your mood.

Time: 5-10 minutes.

Tools: Watering can.

How: Check the soil moisture of your plants. Water each plant as needed, ensuring you do not overwater.

How did watering your plants affect your mood and the ambiance of your space?

323. Play background music

Why: Playing background music can create a pleasant atmosphere and improve your mood. It helps you relax and focus on your tasks.

Time: 5-10 minutes.

Tools: Music player or streaming service.

How: Choose calming or inspiring music. Set the volume to a comfortable level and let it play in the background while you go about your activities.

How did playing background music affect your mood and focus?

324. Change your pillowcases

Why: Fresh pillowcases can improve your sleep quality and comfort. It makes your bed feel clean and inviting.

Time: 5-10 minutes.

Tools: Clean pillowcases.

How: Remove the old pillowcases from your pillows. Replace them with fresh, clean ones, ensuring they are snugly fitted.

How did changing your pillowcases affect your sleep quality and comfort?

325. Scent your space with essential oils

Why: Adding a pleasant scent to your space can improve your mood. It creates a relaxing and inviting environment.

Time: 5-10 minutes.

Tools: Essential oils, diffuser.

How: Fill your diffuser with water and add a few drops of your favorite essential oil. Turn on the diffuser and let the scent fill the room. Alternatively, use a spray bottle to mist the room with a diluted essential oil mixture.

How did scenting your space affect your mood and the ambiance of the room?

326. Add a candle to your bathroom

Why: Adding a candle can create a relaxing atmosphere in your bathroom. It makes your space more inviting and enhances your self-care routine.

Time: 5-10 minutes.

Tools: Scented candle.

How: Choose a scented candle that you find relaxing. Place it on a safe surface in your bathroom and light it during your self-care routines like baths or skincare.

How did adding a candle to your bathroom affect your ability to unwind and de-stress?

327. Open curtains to maximize natural light

Why: Opening curtains to let in natural light can enhance your mood and visibility. It creates a brighter and more pleasant environment.

Time: 5-10 minutes.

Tools: None.

How: Open the curtains or blinds in your room to let in as much natural light as possible. Adjust any furniture or decor that may be blocking the light.

How did maximizing natural light in your space affect your mood and energy levels?

328. Clean a bathroom mirror

Why: Cleaning a bathroom mirror can make your space look brighter and more inviting. It improves visibility and enhances the overall look of your bathroom.

Time: 5-10 minutes.

Tools: Glass cleaner, microfiber cloth.

How: Spray glass cleaner on the mirror and wipe it clean with a microfiber cloth. Ensure there are no streaks left behind.

How did cleaning your bathroom mirror affect your perception of cleanliness and brightness in your space?

329. Replace an air freshener

Why: Replacing an old air freshener can make your space smell fresh and pleasant. It enhances the overall atmosphere and comfort of your home.

Time: 5-10 minutes.

Tools: New air freshener.

How: Remove the old air freshener and dispose of it. Replace it with a new one in a scent you enjoy.

How did replacing an air freshener affect the smell and ambiance of your space?

330. Organize your desk drawer

Why: Having an organized desk drawer makes it easier to find what you need. It creates a tidy and efficient workspace, reducing daily stress.

Time: 10-20 minutes.

Tools: None.

How: Empty the drawer completely. Sort items into categories (e.g., stationery, documents). Discard or relocate items you no longer need, then neatly arrange the remaining items back into the drawer.

How did organizing your desk drawer affect your productivity and stress levels?

331. Rearrange a small area

Why: Rearranging a small area can refresh the look of your space. It can boost your mood and make the space feel new.

Time: 10-20 minutes.

Tools: None.

How: Select a small area like a shelf, side table, or corner. Rearrange the items to create a new look, considering functionality and aesthetics.

How did rearranging a small area affect your enjoyment of the space?

332.   Adjust the lighting in one room

Why: Proper lighting can enhance your mood and improve visibility. Adjusting the lighting makes your space more comfortable and pleasant.

Time: 10-20 minutes.

Tools: Light bulbs, lamps.

How: Assess the current lighting in your room. Change light bulbs to a warmer or cooler tone if needed, add lamps or adjust window coverings to let in more natural light.

How did adjusting the lighting affect your comfort and productivity in the space?

333.   Organize digital files

Why: Organizing digital files reduces clutter and makes it easier to find important documents. It helps you feel more in control of your digital space.

Time: 10-20 minutes.

Tools: Computer.

How: Open your digital file manager. Create folders and subfolders to categorize your files. Move files into their appropriate folders and delete any unnecessary files.

How did organizing your digital files affect your stress levels and productivity?

334.   Create a comfort corner with a blanket and pillow

Why: A comfort corner provides a cozy space to relax. It enhances comfort and gives you a dedicated spot to unwind.

Time: 10-20 minutes.

Tools: Blanket, pillow.

How: Choose a quiet corner in your room. Place a soft blanket and a comfortable pillow there, creating a cozy nook for reading, resting, or meditating.

How did creating a comfort corner affect your ability to relax and unwind?

335.   Hang one piece of inspirational art

Why: Inspirational art can boost your motivation and make your space more personal. It adds visual interest and positivity to your environment.

Time: 10-20 minutes.

Tools: Art piece, nails or adhesive hooks.

How: Select a piece of inspirational art. Use nails or adhesive hooks to hang it in a place where you will see it often, such as above your desk or in your bedroom.

How did hanging inspirational art affect your mood and motivation?

336. Color code a set of files

Why: Color coding files can make it easier to find important documents. It helps keep your paperwork organized and accessible.

Time: 10-20 minutes.

Tools: Colored folders or labels.

How: Gather your files and sort them into categories. Assign a color to each category and place the documents into corresponding colored folders or use labels to mark them.

How did color coding your files affect your efficiency and organization?

337. Adjust your chair for better ergonomics

Why: Adjusting your chair can reduce physical strain and increase comfort. It helps prevent discomfort and improves posture while working.

Time: 10-20 minutes.

Tools: Adjustable chair.

How: Adjust the height of your chair so that your feet are flat on the floor and your knees are at a 90-degree angle. Ensure your back is supported and your desk is at elbow height.

How did adjusting your chair affect your comfort and productivity?

338. Add one goal to your vision board

Why: Adding a goal to your vision board helps you stay focused on your aspirations. It serves as a visual reminder of what you want to achieve.

Time: 10-20 minutes.

Tools: Vision board, magazines, scissors, glue.

How: Look through magazines for images and words that represent your new goal. Cut them out and glue them onto your vision board, placing them where they are easily visible.

How did adding to your vision board affect your motivation and focus on your goals?

339. Sort clothes in one drawer

Why: Sorting clothes in one drawer can simplify your wardrobe. It makes it easier to find what you need and reduces clutter.

Time: 10-20 minutes.

Tools: None.

How: Empty the drawer and sort your clothes into keep, donate, and discard piles. Neatly fold and organize the clothes you are keeping and place them back into the drawer.

How did sorting your clothes affect your daily routine and stress levels?

340.   Set up a small recycling bin

Why: Setting up a recycling bin helps you manage waste more effectively. It promotes environmental responsibility and keeps your space organized.

Time: 10-20 minutes.

Tools: Recycling bin, labels.

How: Choose a bin for recycling and place it in a convenient location. Label it clearly and educate household members on what can be recycled.

How did setting up a recycling bin affect your waste management and environmental impact?

341.   Add a welcome mat to your entryway

Why: A welcome mat can make your home feel inviting and keep it cleaner. It sets a positive tone for anyone entering your space.

Time: 10-20 minutes.

Tools: Welcome mat.

How: Select a welcome mat that suits your style. Place it at the entrance of your home to greet guests and reduce dirt tracked inside.

How did adding a welcome mat affect the ambiance of your home?

342. Reorganize a pantry shelf

Why: Reorganizing a pantry shelf can make meal preparation easier. It helps you keep track of what you have and reduces food waste.

Time: 10-20 minutes.

Tools: None.

How: Remove all items from the shelf. Check expiration dates and discard expired items. Group similar items together and place them back on the shelf in an organized manner.

How did reorganizing a pantry shelf affect your meal preparation and food management?

343. Install a desk lamp

Why: A desk lamp provides better lighting for work or reading. It helps reduce eye strain and improves focus.

Time: 10-20 minutes.

Tools: Desk lamp.

How: Choose a desk lamp with adjustable brightness. Place it on your desk and adjust the angle to provide adequate lighting for your tasks.

How did installing a desk lamp affect your productivity and comfort?

344. Label storage bins

Why: Labeling storage bins can improve organization and make finding items easier. It helps keep your space tidy and efficient.

Time: 10-20 minutes.

Tools: Labels, markers.

How: Gather your storage bins and decide what will go in each one. Write clear labels for each bin and attach them. Organize your items into the labeled bins.

How did labeling your storage bins affect your organization and ease of finding items?

345. Plant one herb in a pot

Why: Planting an herb provides fresh ingredients for cooking and adds greenery to your space. It can be a rewarding and relaxing activity.

Time: 10-20 minutes.

Tools: Small pot, soil, herb seeds or seedlings.

How: Fill a small pot with soil and plant your chosen herb seeds or seedlings. Water the plant and place it on a sunny windowsill.

How did planting a herb in your kitchen affect your cooking and the ambiance of your space?

346. Unfollow unnecessary social media accounts

Why: Unfollowing unnecessary accounts can reduce digital clutter and improve mental health. It helps create a more positive and inspiring online environment.

Time: 10-20 minutes.

Tools: Smartphone or computer.

How: Open your social media accounts and review the accounts you follow. Unfollow or mute accounts that do not add value to your life.

How did detoxing your social media feeds affect your mental health and online experience?

347. Set up a cozy reading chair

Why: Setting up a cozy reading chair creates a dedicated space for relaxation and reading. It enhances your comfort and encourages you to take breaks.

Time: 10-20 minutes.

Tools: Comfortable chair, good lighting.

How: Choose a comfortable chair and place it in a quiet area. Add a soft blanket or cushion and ensure there is good lighting for reading.

How did setting up a cozy reading chair affect your ability to relax and enjoy reading?

348. Add seasonal decor to a table

Why: Refreshing your space with seasonal decor can make it feel more festive and welcoming. It adds visual interest and reflects the current season.

Time: 10-20 minutes.

Tools: Seasonal decor items.

How: Choose a table or surface to decorate. Add a few seasonal items like a small pumpkin, a vase of fresh flowers, or holiday decorations.

How did adding seasonal decor affect the ambiance of your home?

349. Reorganize a section of your bookshelf

Why: Reorganizing a section of your bookshelf can make your space look tidier and more organized. It makes it easier to find and enjoy your books.

Time: 10-20 minutes.

Tools: None.

How: Remove books from a section of your shelf. Sort them by genre, author, or color and place them back in an organized manner.

How did reorganizing your bookshelf affect your enjoyment of your space?

350. Hang a bulletin board

Why: A bulletin board keeps important notes and reminders in one place. It helps you stay organized and on top of tasks.

Time: 10-20 minutes.

Tools: Bulletin board, nails or adhesive hooks.

How: Select a spot to hang your bulletin board. Use nails or adhesive hooks to secure it to the wall. Pin important notes, reminders, and inspirational quotes.

How did hanging a bulletin board affect your organization and efficiency?

351. Tidy up your craft supplies

Why: Keeping your craft supplies organized can boost your creativity and make projects more enjoyable. It saves time searching for materials.

Time: 10-20 minutes.

Tools: None.

How: Gather all your craft supplies. Sort them into categories and store them in labeled containers or drawers.

How did tidying up your craft supplies affect your creativity and productivity?

352.   Place a cushion in a quiet corner for meditation

Why: Setting up a meditation corner provides a dedicated space for mindfulness. It enhances relaxation and focus.

Time: 10-20 minutes.

Tools: Cushion, soft lighting.

How: Find a quiet corner in your home. Place a comfortable cushion and add soft lighting or candles to create a serene atmosphere.

How did setting up a meditation corner affect your ability to relax and meditate?

353.   Hang a photo on your wall

Why: Hanging a photo personalizes your space and brings joy. It adds a touch of warmth and memories to your environment.

Time: 10-20 minutes.

Tools: Photo, frame, nails or adhesive hooks.

How: Choose a favorite photo and frame it. Use nails or adhesive hooks to hang it in a spot where you will see it often.

How did hanging a photo affect your sense of connection and happiness in your space?

354. Organize your shoe rack

Why: An organized shoe rack can simplify your daily routine and keep your space tidy. It makes it easier to find and access your shoes.

Time: 10-20 minutes.

Tools: None.

How: Remove all shoes from the rack. Sort them by type or frequency of use and place them back neatly. Discard or donate any shoes you no longer wear.

How did organizing your shoe rack affect your daily routine and the tidiness of your space?

355. Wipe down kitchen counters

Why: Clean kitchen counters can make your space look and feel more hygienic. It provides a clear and pleasant area for meal preparation.

Time: 10-20 minutes.

Tools: All-purpose cleaner, sponge or cloth.

How: Spray all-purpose cleaner on your kitchen counters. Wipe them down thoroughly with a sponge or cloth, removing any crumbs or spills.

How did wiping down your kitchen counters affect your sense of cleanliness and readiness for cooking?

356. Clean out your wallet or purse

Why: Cleaning out your wallet or purse can reduce clutter and make it easier to find essentials. It helps you stay organized and avoid carrying unnecessary items.

Time: 10-20 minutes.

Tools: None.

How: Empty your wallet or purse. Remove old receipts and unnecessary items. Organize your cards, cash, and essential items back into their designated spots.

How did cleaning out your wallet or purse affect your organization and daily convenience?

357. Vacuum one room

Why: Vacuuming can make your space feel cleaner and fresher. It improves air quality and removes dirt and dust from your floors.

Time: 10-20 minutes.

Tools: Vacuum cleaner.

How: Plug in your vacuum cleaner and vacuum the entire floor of one room. Focus on corners and under furniture where dust tends to accumulate.

How did vacuuming one room affect your perception of cleanliness and comfort in your space?

358. Organize your spice rack

Why: An organized spice rack can make cooking more efficient and enjoyable. It helps you quickly find the spices you need and keeps your kitchen tidy.

Time: 10-20 minutes.

Tools: None.

How: Remove all spices from the rack. Sort them alphabetically or by frequency of use and place them back in an orderly fashion.

How did organizing your spice rack affect your cooking experience and the tidiness of your kitchen?

359. Clean a light fixture

Why: Cleaning a light fixture can brighten your space and improve lighting. It enhances the overall appearance of your room.

Time: 10-20 minutes.

Tools: Glass cleaner, microfiber cloth.

How: Turn off the light and remove any dust or dirt from the fixture. Use glass cleaner and a microfiber cloth to clean the glass parts.

How did cleaning a light fixture affect the brightness and ambiance of your space?

360. Organize your desk supplies

Why: Organizing your desk supplies can boost productivity and reduce clutter. It makes it easier to find what you need and keeps your workspace tidy.

Time: 10-20 minutes.

Tools: Containers or organizers.

How: Gather all your desk supplies. Sort them into categories (e.g., pens, paper clips) and store them in containers or organizers. Place them back on your desk in an orderly manner.

How did organizing your desk supplies affect your productivity and the tidiness of your workspace?

361. Organize your jewelry

Why: Keeping your jewelry organized can save time and reduce stress when getting ready. It helps you find and enjoy your pieces more easily.

Time: 10-20 minutes.

Tools: Jewelry organizer or containers.

How: Gather all your jewelry. Sort it into categories (e.g., rings, necklaces) and store it in an organizer or containers. Place them in a designated area for easy access.

How did organizing your jewelry affect your ability to find and enjoy your pieces?

362. Clean a window

Why: Cleaning a window can make your space look brighter and more inviting. It improves visibility and enhances the overall appearance of your room.

Time: 10-20 minutes.

Tools: Glass cleaner, microfiber cloth.

How: Spray glass cleaner on the window and wipe it clean with a microfiber cloth. Ensure there are no streaks left behind.

How did cleaning a window affect the brightness and ambiance of your space?

363. Create a relaxation playlist

Why: A relaxation playlist can help you unwind and reduce stress. Listening to calming music can improve your mood and create a soothing atmosphere.

Time: 20-30 minutes.

Tools: Music player or streaming service.

How: Open your music app and search for calming songs or playlists. Add your favorite tracks to a new playlist. Listen to this playlist during relaxation times like reading or before bed.

How did curating and listening to a relaxation playlist affect your stress levels and relaxation?

364. Draw or paint a small art piece

Why: Creating a small art piece can boost your creativity and personalize your space. It provides a sense of accomplishment and a unique touch to your home.

Time: 20-30 minutes.

Tools: Art supplies.

How: Choose a small canvas or piece of paper. Use paints, markers, or other art supplies to create a simple design or picture. Display your finished artwork in your space.

How did creating a small art piece affect your creativity and sense of accomplishment?

365. Set up a small home office area

Why: Creating a dedicated home office space can improve your productivity and focus. It provides a comfortable and organized area for work or hobbies.

Time: 20-30 minutes.

Tools: Desk, chair, office supplies.

How: Choose a quiet area to set up your home office. Arrange a desk and chair, and organize your office supplies in a neat and accessible manner.

How did setting up a home office area affect your productivity and focus?

CHAPTER 13

SELF-CARE: A LIFELONG COMMITMENT

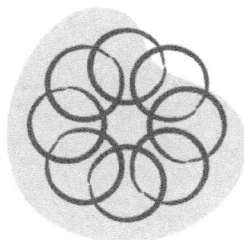

Self-care is fundamental to thriving in life. This book has journeyed through 365 unique self-care activities, showing paths to well-being within your busy life. This is the beginning of a practice that will evolve as you do, a practice essential to your growth and happiness.

Just as we need air to breathe, self-care is essential for maintaining mental, emotional, and physical health. It is not selfish; it is necessary.

By choosing self-care, you reclaim agency over your health and happiness. It is a decisive step toward a balanced life where your needs are equally prioritized.

A Lifelong Journey

Whether it's a five-minute meditation or an hour-long yoga session, the activities you've explored are designed to fit seamlessly into your life, no matter how hectic your schedule.

As your life changes, so will your self-care needs. What works today may not work tomorrow, so be open to adapting your routines to fit your evolving circumstances.

Try different activities to find what truly helps you relax, rejuvenate, and recharge. Keep what works and modify what doesn't. Because if you don't take responsibility for your own care, nobody else will. It's up to you to ensure that self-care remains a constant in your life.

Remember that self-care is not about taking from others—it's about replenishing your own well to continue caring for others effectively.

Recognize that caring for yourself is part of how you show love and responsibility toward those dependent on you.

The Path Forward

As you move forward, keep the self-care goals you set in Chapter 2 in mind. Are they realistic? Do they still align with your needs?

Adapt them as necessary so they continue to serve you well. Every step you take on this path strengthens your commitment to a healthier, more joyful life.

The journey of self-care is one of the most profound commitments you can make—to yourself and by extension, to those you love. May you walk it with courage, curiosity, and compassion.

And if this book has helped you in any way, please leave a review to help other women like you find it and get as empowered by it.

All the best on your self-care journey!

-Sandy Ross.

RESOURCES AND REFERENCES

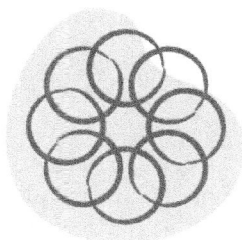

Discover More Self-Care Resources

Your journey toward self-care doesn't end with this book. It's important to have access to ongoing support and additional resources to help you maintain and evolve your self-care practices. To provide you with the best and most up-to-date information, we've created a dedicated resource page on our website.

Visit our resource page for recommended reading, links to helpful videos, apps and podcasts, and our free worksheets.

Simply visit www.SandyRossAuthor.com/resources to explore these valuable resources and more.

We update this page regularly to ensure you always have the most current and useful information at your fingertips.

Remember, self-care is a lifelong journey, and you don't have to walk it alone. Let our resource page be your companion in cultivating a healthier, happier you.

References

Bal PM, et al. (2013). How does fiction reading influence empathy? An experimental investigation on the role of emotional transportation. http://www.ncbi.nlm.nih.gov/pubmed/23383160

Barton J, et al. (2010) What is the best dose of nature and green exercise for improving mental health? A multi-study analysis. https://pubmed.ncbi.nlm.nih.gov/20337470/

Blancheflower DG, et al. (2012). Is psychological well-being linked to the consumption of fruit and vegetables? https://warwick.ac.uk/fac/soc/economics/research/workingpapers/2012/twerp_996.pdf

Bialowolski, P., Weziak-Bialowolska, D., Lee, M. T., Chen, Y., VanderWeele, T. J., & McNeely, E. (2021). The role of financial conditions for physical and mental health. Evidence from a longitudinal survey and insurance claims data. Social Science & Medicine, 281, 114041. https://doi.org/10.1016/j.socscimed.2021.114041

Gump BB, et al, (2000). Are vacations good for your health? The 9-year mortality experience after the multiple risk factor intervention trial. http://www.ncbi.nlm.nih.gov/pubmed/11020089

Keng, S., Smoski, M. J., & Robins, C. J. (2011). Effects of mindfulness on psychological health: A review of empirical studies. Clinical Psychology Review, 31(6), 1041-1056. https://doi.org/10.1016/j.cpr.2011.04.006

Mahindru, A., Patil, P., & Agrawal, V. (2023). Role of physical activity on mental health and well-being: A review. Cureus. https://doi.org/10.7759/cureus.33475

Schmid, J., Imbach, L., Klaperski, S., & Sudeck, G. (2021). The natural environment of physical activity and perceived stress: The mediating role of specific recovery experiences. Frontiers in Sports and Active Living, 3. https://doi.org/10.3389/fspor.2021.706467

Schneiderman, N., Ironson, G., & Siegel, S. D. (2005). Stress and health: Psychological, behavioral, and biological determinants. Annual Review of Clinical Psychology, 1(1), 607-628. https://doi.org/10.1146/annurev.clinpsy.1.102803.144141

Self care industry statistics: Market data report 2024. (2024, July 23). Worldmetrics.org: Statistics & Reports. https://worldmetrics.org/self-care-industry-statistics/

Simkus, E., Chielli, D., & Merlo, G. (2022). Self-care, including the history of the nurses' code. Lifestyle Nursing, 145-151. https://doi.org/10.1201/9781003178330-11

Stephens R, et al. (2011). Swearing as a response to pain-effect of daily swearing frequency. http://www.ncbi.nlm.nih.gov/pubmed/22078790

Umberson, D., & Karas Montez, J. (2010). Social relationships and health: A flashpoint for health policy. Journal of Health and Social Behavior, 51(1_suppl), S54-S66. https://doi.org/10.1177/0022146510383501

Wang, Z., Liu, H., Yu, H., Wu, Y., Chang, S., & Wang, L. (2017). Associations between occupational stress, burnout and well-being among manufacturing workers: Mediating roles of psychological capital and self-esteem. BMC Psychiatry, 17(1). https://doi.org/10.1186/s12888-017-1533-6

Boecker H, et al. (2008). The runner's high: Opioidergic mechanisms in the human brain. https://academic.oup.com/cercor/article/18/11/2523/291108

Campos D, et al. (2019). Exploring the role of meditation and dispositional mindfulness on social cognition domains: A controlled study https://www.ncbi.nlm.nih.gov/pmc/articles/PMC6470267/

Carlson E. (2013). Overcoming the barriers to self-knowledge: Mindfulness as a path to seeing yourself as you really are. https://journals.sagepub.com/doi/abs/10.1177/1745691612462584

Coon Thompson J, et al. (2011). Does participating in physical activity in outdoor natural environments have a greater effect on physical and mental wellbeingwell-being than physical activity indoors? A systematic review. https://pubmed.ncbi.nlm.nih.gov/21291246/

Fredrickson BL, et al. (2013). A functional genomic perspective on human well-being. http://www.ncbi.nlm.nih.gov/pmc/articles/PMC3746929/

Hirosaki M, et al. (2013). Effects of a laughter and exercise program on physiological and psychological health among community-dwelling elderly in Japan: randomized controlled trial. http://www.ncbi.nlm.nih.gov/pubmed/22672359

Hyunju J, et al. (2019). Physiological benefits of viewing nature: A systematic review of indoor experiments. https://www.ncbi.nlm.nih.gov/pmc/articles/PMC6926748/

Jenkinson CE, et al. (2013). Is volunteering a public health intervention? A systematic review and meta-analysis of the health and survival of volunteers. https://pubmed.ncbi.nlm.nih.gov/23968220/

Kuyken W, et al. (2013). Effectiveness of the mindfulness in schools programme: non-randomised controlled feasibility study. https://www.cambridge.org/core/journals/the-british-journal-of-psychiatry/article/effectiveness-of-the-mindfulness-in-schools-programme-nonrandomised-controlled-feasibility-study/BEB4925E41DEB31345A4FB14FA264A09

Labrique-Walusis F, et al. (2010). Massage therapy for stress management: implications for nursing practice. http://www.ncbi.nlm.nih.gov/pubmed/20664464

Ma K, et al. (2016). Mood migration: How enfacing a smile makes you happier. https://pubmed.ncbi.nlm.nih.gov/26970854/

Miller M, et al. (2010). Divergent effects of joyful and anxiety-provoking music on endothelial vasoreactivity. http://www.ncbi.nlm.nih.gov/pubmed/20368475

Mills A, et al. (2019). Helping students to self-care and enhance their health-promotion skills. https://pubmed.ncbi.nlm.nih.gov/31303044/

Mohan A, et al. (2011). Effect of meditation on stress-induced changes in cognitive functions. https://pubmed.ncbi.nlm.nih.gov/21417807/

Mrazek MD, et al. (2013). Mindfulness training improves working memory capacity and GRE performance while reducing mind wandering. https://pubmed.ncbi.nlm.nih.gov/23538911/

Muller-Pinget S, et al. (2012). Dance therapy improves self-body image among obese patients. http://www.ncbi.nlm.nih.gov/pubmed/23031613

Murphy MLM, et al. (2018). Receiving a hug is associated with the attenuation of negative mood that occurs on days with interpersonal conflict. https://www.ncbi.nlm.nih.gov/pmc/articles/PMC6169869/

Obasi CN, et al. (2013). Advantage of meditation over exercise in reducing cold and flu illness is related to improved function and quality of life. https://www.ncbi.nlm.nih.gov/pmc/articles/PMC3582749/

Richardson S. (2012). Meta-analysis of perceived stress and its association with incident coronary heart disease. http://www.ncbi.nlm.nih.gov/pubmed/22975465

Ritter SM, et al. (2017). Happy creativity: Listening to happy music facilitates divergent thinking. https://pubmed.ncbi.nlm.nih.gov/28877176/

Stephens R, et al. (2011). Swearing as a response to pain-effect of daily swearing frequency. http://www.ncbi.nlm.nih.gov/pubmed/22078790.

Steptoe A, et al. (2005). Positive affect and health-related neuroendocrine, cardiovascular, and inflammatory processes. http://www.ncbi.nlm.nih.gov/pmc/articles/PMC1088362/

Subhani M, et al. (2011). New Article of Clothing translates the Mood of an Individual. http://www.ijbssnet.com/journals/Vol_2_No_23_Special_Issue_December_2011/21.pdf

Sugawara J, et al. (2010). Effect of mirthful laughter on vascular function. https://pubmed.ncbi.nlm.nih.gov/20816128/

Verghese J, et al. (2003). Leisure activities and the risk of dementia in the elderly.https://www.nejm.org/doi/full/10.1056/NEJMoa022252#t=articleResults a

Wilson RS, et al. (2013). Life-span cognitive activity, neuropathologic burden, and cognitive aging. https://n.neurology.org/content/81/4/314

ABOUT SANDY ROSS

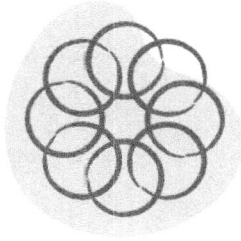

Sandy Ross is a counselor and wellness advocate dedicated to promoting holistic health and empowerment. Her book, *365 Self-Care Activities for Women*, was inspired by her professional experiences with clients who struggled to find time for self-care and her personal journey in managing her own wellbeing.

Sandy noticed a significant need for accessible, practical resources that could help integrate self-care into busy lives, leading her to compile a year's worth of easy-to-follow daily activities. Through this book, she aims to empower women to take charge of their well-being by providing strategies that are both actionable and beneficial.

Find more self-care and well-being resources at her website, www.SandyRossAuthor.com.

Printed in Great Britain
by Amazon